STRATEGIC MARKETING

Official Module Guide

The Chartered Institute of Marketing
Moor Hall
Cookham
Maidenhead
Berkshire
SL6 9QH
United Kingdom

www.cim.co.uk

First published 2014

Revised edition published 2017

A catalogue record for this book is available from the British Library.

ISBN 978-1-9073-68-33-2 (paperback)
ISBN 978-1-907368-37-0 (ebook)

CONTENTS

1

2

MARKETING IS CONSTANTLY EVOLVING AND IT'S IMPORTANT TO DEMONSTRATE YOU HAVE KEPT UP TO DATE WITH THE LATEST DEVELOPMENTS.

Following extensive research among marketing professionals and the wider business community we launched a portfolio of award-based qualifications to reflect the market need for flexible bite-sized learning for today's professional marketer.

Each individual module can be achieved as a distinct self-contained award and, when combined with further awards, built into a full qualification if and when required.

Each module is based on our unique Professional Marketing Competencies, designed to help you meet the ever-increasing demands on expected of marketers at every stage of their career.

CIM (The Chartered Institute of Marketing) is the leading international professional marketing body. CIM exists to develop the marketing profession, maintain professional standards and improve the skills of marketing practitioners, enabling them to deliver exceptional results for their organisations.

Our range of professional qualifications and training programmes – along with our extensive membership benefits – are all designed to support you, develop your knowledge, enable you to grow, and increase your network. Our professional pathway will help you excel and realise your full potential.

PROFESSIONAL MARKETING COMPETENCIES

The Professional Marketing Competencies are a framework that provide a guide to the skills and behaviours that are expected of professional marketers at varying levels of proficiency.

Developed from extensive research with employers and employees in marketing and broader business functions, the Professional Marketing Competencies give individuals and organisations the basis on which to assess the abilities of a capable and competent marketer.

More information about the Professional Marketing Competencies can be found on our website: www.cim.co.uk/competencies

THE PROFESSIONAL MARKETING COMPETENCIES

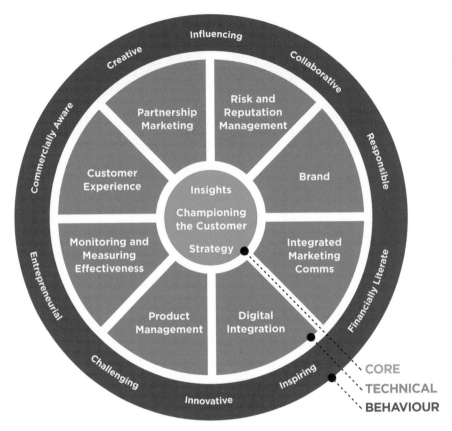

© CIM 2016

QUALIFICATION OVERVIEW

The Diploma in Professional Marketing gives you the knowledge, skills and understanding at management level to enable you to take a strategic approach to marketing planning. By understanding key marketing metrics and measurement techniques you will be able to interpret relevant insight and make informed strategic decisions.

1. INTRODUCTION TO THE MODULE

Strategic Marketing is a mandatory module that sits within the suite of Diploma modules. To gain the CIM Diploma in Professional Marketing you need to pass this and the Marketing Metrics mandatory module, plus one elective module – either Driving Innovation or Digital Strategy. However, you will gain a module award for each individual module you pass.

2. MODULE CONTENT

This module is about how to take a strategic approach to marketing planning in order to help your organisation achieve competitive advantage. It recognises the significance of situation analysis and introduces techniques for assessing the external and internal environments that enable effective decision-making. It outlines the importance of all stages within the marketing planning process, from the audit, through strategic decision-making, to implementation of plans. And it explains how managing resources and using monitoring and measurement techniques enables the marketer to achieve strategic marketing objectives. The module is not an introduction to the marketing planning process, but is intended to build on existing knowledge gained either from previous study or from working as a practitioner.

3. BENEFITS OF STUDYING THE MODULE

Strong strategic marketing plans are at the heart of successful businesses and anyone aspiring to a senior position in marketing or elsewhere in their organisation needs to understand and master strategy. The concepts and ideas covered in this module will enable you to think about marketing planning from a strategic perspective, something that is critical in being able to talk the same language as senior management and see the bigger picture for the organisation. In the current volatile environment, strategy is about being able to manage uncertainty, so many of the concepts we look at in this module will give you practical tools and techniques to help you do this. The model will also help you to take a critical view of some of the more traditional marketing ideas and concepts and help you assess some of the newer theories and practices.

4. PLAN YOUR JOURNEY

This study guide is part of a module toolkit, which comprises a wide range of study resources available to you. No single resource is sufficient to gain a full understanding of the module content, and this study guide is intended to provide you with a brief overview of the content of the module and act as a bridge to further resources.

Each chapter looks at a specific set of tools and concepts and is directly linked to the syllabus content for each of the six learning outcomes for this module. The study guide is intended to be used in conjunction with the recommended textbook, but you will also find it valuable to refer to some of the other textbooks mentioned within the guide. See overleaf for more details.

Recommended textbook

Hooley, G., Nicoulaud, B., Piercy, N. and Rudd, J. (2017) *Marketing strategy and competitive positioning.* 6th edition. Harlow, FT Prentice Hall. [ISBN 9781292017310].

Supplementary textbooks

Aaker, D. and McLouglin, D. (2010) *Strategic market management: global perspectives.* Chichester, John Wiley. [ISBN 9780470689752]

Cravens, D.W. and Piercy, N. (2012) *Strategic marketing.* 10th edition. US, McGraw-Hill. [ISBN 9780071326230]

McDonald, M. and Wilson, H. (2016) *Marketing plans: how to prepare them, how to profit from them.* 8th edition. Chichester, John Wiley. [ISBN 9781119217138]

The textbooks cover the topics in this module in much more detail – but they have not been written with the CIM's syllabus in mind. Within each chapter of this study guide you will find references to the recommended textbook, and at the end of each chapter a 'Further reading' section indicating chapters within the recommended text that contain content relevant to the topic covered. There are also references and suggested further reading for the supplementary textbooks.

In addition, the study guide summarises ideas and concepts from a range of key articles in academic journals, many of which are available via the CIM's study website. It is always advisable to read the original paper because it usually provides insights into a theory or case study that a brief summary is unable to do. The study guide also contains a range of short case studies and practical exercises to help you put some of the theories and frameworks into context. In preparing for the examination of this module you will need to apply a range of concepts and tools to a real organisation – so the exercises here will give you some practice and provide solutions against which to assess your answers. Finally, each chapter contains a short quiz to help you consolidate your learning from each chapter.

ASSESSMENTS

The assessment for this module is a three-hour controlled extended-answer examination.

Learners have to produce a marketing plan before the examination, which they will take into the exam and use to respond to the tasks presented. The marketing plan will be based on a brief released six months before the exam and learners must submit it along with their answer book at the end of the exam. The plan will count for 40% of the overall assessment marks.

Both elements of this assessment (marketing plan and exam) will cover 100% of the desired learning outcomes and at least 70% of the associated assessment criteria, which are highlighted as sub-headings within this study guide. Please refer to the module specifications on the website for more detail.

You can find assessment criteria and a sample assessment within the Strategic Marketing module specification in the MyCIM section of the CIM website www.cim.co.uk.

RECOMMENDED BOOK

The recommended text for this module is the 6th edition of Marketing Strategy and Competitive Positioning (2017) by Graham Hooley, Nigel Piercy, Brigitte Nicoulaud and John Rudd. The table below links the chapters in the recommended text to the chapters in the module guide (as far as it is possible to do so).

Module guide chapter	Recommended text chapter title
1. The current and future external environment	• The changing market environment • Customer analysis • Competitor analysis • Understanding the organisational resource base
2. The current and future internal environment	• Understanding the organisational resource base • Strategy implementation and internal marketing
3. Using analysis and information to inform strategic decision making	• Strategic marketing planning
4. Developing strategic marketing plans	• Strategic marketing planning • Segmentation and positioning principles
5. Managing resources to deliver the strategic marketing plan	• Creating sustainable competitive advantage
6. Monitor, measure, and adapt the marketing plan to drive continuous improvement	• Competing through superior service and customer relationships

MyCIM
CIM itself offers a variety of resources to all its members, including Student Resources, Marketing Expert, MyiLibrary, Ebsco and Emerald. You can find these at www.cim.co.uk within MyCIM.

Student Resources
These are guides to help you delve deeper into material that supports the six learning outcomes in this module. The links are taken from CIM material, and include links to Marketing Expert, Content Hub, Ebsco and Emerald as well as other resources that will help your learning journey.

Marketing Expert and Content Hub
Marketing Expert has a range of practical guides, templates, topic guides and legal notes on marketing. Content Hub has blogs, editorials, podcasts, webinars on the wide range of marketing topics.

MyiLibrary
The library at Moor Hall is open to all learners Monday to Friday between the hours of 9am and 5pm. For those who can't get to it, MyiLibrary is a good alternative. It allows you to read a range of marketing books on your desktop, and, in some cases, you can download them to your e-reader for seven days.

Ebsco and Emerald
Ebsco is an online database of reference material that is updated every day. It includes journals, magazines, newspapers and reports covering all aspects of marketing and business from around the world.

Learners also have full access to the Emerald marketing eJournal collection. An online user guide provides a detailed list of current titles and information on how to search the collection. It also contains a range of older editions that the library has subscribed to historically.

Remember, all of this information is available via MyCIM.

Marketing news

Finally, one further way you can develop your knowledge and understanding is to keep up to date with what's going on in the real world of marketing. All members can access *Catalyst, our magazine,* free, but magazines such as *Campaign, Marketing Week* and *The Drum* provide a wealth of informative, insightful and fascinating information, augmented by up-to-date opinion, blogs, stories and resources on their websites. You could also follow the hundreds of publishers, marketing theorists, academics, companies, brands and agencies who post content on social media.

Or you could take advantage of *Cutting Edge*, the CIM's weekly digest of short and snappy marketing-related news items from across the sectors, available at www.cim.co.uk/cuttingedge when logged into MyCIM.

Please note: All information included in this Introduction was correct at the time of going to print. Please check the Study Connect e-newsletters for any updates or changes.

1.

SITUATION ANALYSIS: THE CURRENT AND FUTURE EXTERNAL ENVIRONMENT

OUTLINE

This chapter will help you to understand how to analyse an organisation's current and future external environment. At the end of this chapter you will be able to:

- Explain the relationship between market orientation, analysing the external environment and creating value-delivering strategies.
- Understand how to apply a range of marketing analysis techniques across an organisation's external environment in order to generate market insights.
- Recognise the significance of, and problems associated with, analysing an organisation's external environment.

DEFINITIONS

Market orientation – "A culture which encourages behaviour that creates value for the customer leading to superior performance for the business." (Narver and Slater, 1990)

Competitive advantage – The way in which an organisation can satisfy customer needs better than its rivals and earn above-average profits.

Sustainable competitive advantage – Superiority over market rivals that persists long term and is hard for competitors to overcome.

Macro environment – The broad environmental factors that are external to an organisation's market and industry.

Micro environment – The organisation's close external environment, including its competitors, customers, distribution channels, suppliers, complementers (suppliers of complementary products) and other relevant stakeholders.

Industry – A group of organisations producing the same principal product or service.

Market – A group of existing and potential customers for a particular product or service, who have similar needs.

Stakeholder – "Any group or individual who can affect or is affected by the achievement of the firm's objectives." (Freeman, 1984)

'Red oceans' – "Represent all the industries in existence today – the known market space. In red oceans industry boundaries are defined and accepted, and the competitive rules of the game are well understood." (Kim and Mauborgne, 2004)

'Blue oceans' – "Denote all the industries not in existence today – the unknown market space, untainted by competition." (Kim and Mauborgne, 2004)

13

1.1

ORIENTATION, EXTERNAL ANALYSIS AND THE CREATION OF VALUE-DELIVERING STRATEGIES

The increasingly volatile, uncertain, complex and ambiguous (VUCA) nature of markets means that organisations have to be insightful, innovative, adaptable and responsive if they are to survive and prosper. While strategic management looks at the overall direction of the organisation, marketing strategy focuses on the customer. The comments by Rust et al (2010) typify the belief that successful organisations in the current environment are those that put the customer at the heart of their strategy-making processes. This is the logic behind market-driven strategy. One of the key characteristics of this approach to strategy is being market oriented.

Market orientation – Research from 1990 by Kohli and Jaworski and Narver and Slater established the requirements for, along with the benefits (in terms of profitability) of, becoming more market oriented. Developing a market orientation means that the organisation should focus on long-term profits and adopt a strategic rather than a tactical view of the world. Customer value should be at the heart of the organisation's culture and is supported by:

- **Customer orientation** – Which enables the organisation to understand and create value for its customers on a continuous basis.
- **Competitor orientation** – Understanding competitors and their key resources and abilities.
- **Inter-functional co-ordination** – Utilising all the organisation's assets and capabilities to create customer value.

As we will see later in this chapter and in the next chapter, understanding the organisation itself and the market it operates in is central to effective analysis of the external and internal environments. Marketing is best placed to understand customers and competitors as well as the wider environment because of its externally focused nature. Marketing can also analyse effectively a range of internal resources and capabilities – such as brands and new product development.

However, despite the need for inter-functional co-ordination, ensuring that the whole workforce is involved in and supports a market orientation can be difficult because, in some cases, it requires a significant cultural change. Real Life 1.1 opposite illustrates how one company changed its orientation, but the process was led by a new CEO and it took a crisis to trigger the change.

There are a number of alternative orientations that you might encounter in organisations. Among the most common are:

- Sales – **Sales-oriented** organisations are usually dominated by the finance function and tend to take a short-term view and have quarterly profits as a key metric. Marketing is seen as a cost rather than an asset.

- Production – In **production-oriented** companies the manufacturing or operations department is the key player. This is typical of many organisations producing high-volume low-variety products and services.
- Product – **Product-oriented** companies focus on innovation and design. Being first to market is a key objective, but these companies can suffer due to an initially slow response from the market. The Real Life case below demonstrates how damaging this culture can be to an organisation.

REAL LIFE 1.1
LEGO builds a market orientation

When Jørgen Vig Knudstorp took over as CEO of Danish toy maker LEGO in 2004 the company was close to bankruptcy. Although the firm had a strong reputation for innovation and numerous exclusive licensing deals to manufacture film-based toys for blockbusters like *Star Wars*, it had also lost its core identity. Costs had spiralled out of control due to the dominance of the design teams, which had developed new toys that involved production having to manufacture over 12,000 components for LEGO kits compared with just 7,000 a few years before. The design teams had also lost touch with the firm's customers and were producing too many new toys that customers didn't value and that had limited appeal in the marketplace. For example, Galidor action figures and the Clickits building system, which was aimed at girls, had both failed.

The new CEO put in place a new structure to oversee innovation and co-ordinate new product development. This brought together the designers with other teams in the business such as marketing, supply chain and manufacturing. The company took away some of the control from the designers and started to elicit more ideas from LEGO's user communities through an open innovation programme. The company also worked hard to understand the female segment of its market and conducted a programme of intensive market research to generate insights into what girls wanted. It employed anthropologists and ethnographers to watch how children played with prototype toys and this led to the successful launch of LEGO Friends in 2011. At the end of 2013 LEGO overtook Hasbro to become the second largest toy company in the world behind Mattel – evidence that its new strategy had paid off.

Sources: BBC, 2013; License Europe, 2006; Robertson, D. and Hjuler, P., 2009; Weiners, B., 2011; Wallop, H., 2012; Greene, J., 2010; Lego, 2006-2014.

Achieving competitive advantage – Understanding customers and what they value, and having a good knowledge of competitors, are critical in crafting a strategy that will help the organisation to achieve a competitive advantage. Configuring the organisation to meet customer needs then enables it to achieve this result. According to Thompson et al (2013), competitive advantage is achieved by firms that can satisfy customer needs better than rivals. To do this, they need to either provide the product or service at a lower cost or develop products or services that buyers value more highly. Some organisations use their location or technology to offer both, as we will see in Chapter 4. Having a competitive advantage usually leads to higher profits, and if it is a sustainable advantage this can mean that shareholders or other investors will enjoy good returns over a long period of time.

The marketing planning process – All organisations' strategies tend to evolve over time or have an 'emergent' (Mintzberg and Waters, 1985) component to them, yet many still use a formal system for developing their marketing strategy.

Fig 1.1 Generic marketing strategy planning model

There is a range of marketing planning process models that provide basic frameworks for the task, including:

- MOST – Mission, Objectives, Strategy, Tactics.
- P.R. Smith's SOSTAC® – Situation analysis, Objectives, Strategy, Tactics, Actions, and Control.
- APIC – Audit and Analysis, Planning, Implementation, and Evaluation and Control.

In the remainder of this chapter and the next we will focus on the tools, techniques and processes that you will need to carry out the audit/ situation analysis element of a strategic marketing plan. We will also look at some of the problems you may encounter along the way.

Market analysis skills – To conduct an effective evaluation of the external environment an organisation needs staff with the relevant skills and abilities. A continuous approach to scanning the external environment is more likely to give firms a competitive advantage than more formalised planning processes, which can lock them into an annual cycle of market analysis and evaluation. Cravens and Piercy (2012) suggest that organisations need to adopt a market-sensing process and focus on learning in order to respond rapidly to change in the environment. In order to be able to do this, marketers need a range of skills:

- **Judgement** – As more and more information and data is generated about customers and the environment, marketers need to be able to determine the value of the analysis they carry out, whether in terms of the level of threat a competitor poses or the attractiveness of a particular market segment. Judgement is therefore critical.
- **Interpretation** – Marketers need to be able to interpret the mass of data available and discern patterns and trends. This means going beyond simple forecasts and, in some cases, creating compelling narratives that the organisation can buy into.
- **Research** – You need to take a systematic and robust approach to market research to respond both to the mass of data available and the growing sophistication and knowledge of customers. You also need expert knowledge in order to select the appropriate methods and approaches for auditing and analysing your organisation's macro and micro environments.
- **Synthesis** – In order to create a coherent picture of the threats and opportunities in the organisation's external environment, you need to be able to draw together disparate pieces of data and information and discern the inter-relationships between them.
- **Generalisation** – You need to be able to identify both typical cases and outliers from the information you gather and analyse. And because marketing has become more sophisticated, research has to be more sophisticated too. The need to identify segments in

new ways means you will also have to make use of primary data, rather than relying on older techniques such as geodemographics, for example.

- **Shared understanding** – You need to be able to create plans and communicate about markets in a way that the rest of the organisation understands.
- **Concluding** – The results of market analysis need to pass the 'so what?' test – in other words marketers need to draw clear conclusions from their analysis that communicate a call to action to senior managers. Ultimately, all the auditing and analysis that goes into a strategic marketing plan is designed to support the decision-making process that drives what the organisation then actually does.

1.2

Macro environment

As we've seen from the brief coverage of the marketing planning process above, most marketing strategies start with a systematic analysis and assessment of the organisation's external environment. The broader, or macro, environment contains elements that most organisations have either little or no control over, but which have a major impact on their strategy. Marketers have to identify and evaluate the changes that are taking place or likely to occur in the macro environment in order to make robust strategic choices.

The most commonly used tool for analysing this part of the external environment is PEST, which covers political, economic, social and technological factors. There are many variations (PESTELE, PESTEL, STEEPLE, STEP etc), some of which also include legal, environmental, cultural, demographic and ethical factors, but these additional factors can also be incorporated in the four PEST elements.

The key to using the knowledge gained from this analysis effectively is to avoid producing a simple list. The factors are often interrelated and some will have more impact on certain organisations than others. Treating the external environment like an ecosystem leads to more insightful conclusions than producing a long list of factors.

REAL LIFE 1.2

19

Watch the following YouTube video about digital music.

http://www.youtube.com/watch?v=rTGGITsaFdU

In the clip the presenter, Gerd Leonhard, talks extensively about the way in which social and technological factors are interacting in the music industry's macro environment to produce a significant change in the way consumers buy and listen to music. The shift from supplying a product such as a CD or download, to providing a utility-like service – streaming – will have a profound impact on the business models of many of the organisations in this sector.

To navigate the macro environment successfully marketers need to look for trends and uncertainties in each of the factors they analyse. The distinction between trends and uncertainties is an important one as it underpins some of the more advanced analysis techniques such as scenario planning (covered in Chapter 3).

- **Political/legal** trends and uncertainties could include changes to employment laws, environmental protection legislation or taxation policies, as well as more dramatic factors such as wars and terrorist attacks.

- **Economics** covers factors such as interest and inflation rates, unemployment, trends in GNP, and booms and recessions, which, as we saw from the 2008-10 crash, can have a global impact.
- **Social** issues can be everything from demographic trends to changing lifestyles and fashion trends.
- **Technology** is one of the most significant elements in the macro environment for most organisations, but it's not only transformational changes to technology that require a new business model.
- Marketers also have to take into account a number of other trends and factors when analysing the macro environment. For example, **globalisation** affords access to new markets, but it has also introduced new competitors, while mounting concern about the **environmental and ethical** impact of business has driven substantial amounts of regulation at a national and regional level.

CASE STUDY 1.1

Factors driving the future of the motor industry

Investors, new entrants to the industry and established players are all thinking about what the automotive sector will look like in five, ten or even 20 years' time, and which technologies (and companies) they should back in an increasingly complex and volatile world. There have been many new developments in recent years that provide clues to the future of car manufacturing and driving.

Google has already demonstrated a prototype driverless car, which was able to take a blind man to a drive-through takeaway, and CEO Sergey Brin predicts that these cars will be on the production line within five or six years. New technologies are also changing the way cars are manufactured. Much of the interest in alternative propulsion systems has been driven by increased regulation and tough targets for CO_2 emissions for new vehicles in Europe, parts of Asia (China and Japan) and the United States. The International Energy Agency is forecasting that sales of diesel and petrol cars will peak at around 70 million units in 2020, after which hybrid, LPG, hydrogen fuel cell and even fully electric vehicles will make up an increasing proportion of sales. Forecasts for the growth of electric vehicles vary widely. Enthusiasts such as the CEO of Nissan, Carlos, Ghosn, are predicting that electric vehicles could make up 10% of global vehicle sales by 2020.

Many governments see car manufacturing as a key industry, both because of the supply chains and direct employment it supports and as a flagship for national power. As car sales declined in the late 2000s several governments supported the industry through state-funded scrappage schemes, which have been credited with sustaining or even growing demand. Governments are also having a longer-term impact on the industry through a range of other measures. Targets for CO_2 emissions have been one of the driving factors in the design and production of cleaner cars. The European Union's 'Euro 6' standards, in force from 2014, represent some of the world's strictest standards for petrol and diesel car emissions.

A recent study by First Research stated that the automotive industry is also significantly affected by changes in oil prices and interest rates. As most people use loans to buy cars, there is an obvious link between demand and interest rates. Raw material prices are another important factor for manufacturers. According to First Research, the materials used to manufacture a car in the US account for 70% of its selling price. So changes to the price of oil and its derivatives used in paints and plastics, as well as the cost of metals, such as steel and aluminium, can have a profound impact on the viability of both motor manufacturers and their suppliers.

One trend that is causing considerable concern to car manufacturers is the decline in car ownership among young people in Europe and North America. A recent study by IHS Automotive and Groupe Futuribles found that the number of 16-to-19-year-olds holding driving licences in 2008 was nearly 20% lower than in 1998. However, a counter-trend is the substantial growth in many developing markets, such as China and Brazil, where an expanding middle class are becoming new car owners. Since 2005 China has seen average annual growth in car sales of 26%, with latest figures showing 16% growth in the first quarter of 2013 alone.

Sources: BBC News, 2010; BMI, 2012; First Research, 2013; Forth A., 2013a; Forth, A., 2013b; Gott, P., 2008; Kekic, L. and Nichols, A., 2013; Schumpeter, 2012; The Economist, 2013a; The Economist, 2013b; The Economist, 2013c; The Economist, 2013d; The Economist, 2013e.

ACTIVITY 1.1

Using the case study above list the key factors in the automotive industry's macro environment that are likely to have an impact on firms in this sector over the next five to ten years. How are these factors interrelated? Rate each of the factors you have identified relative to the others, perhaps by using a scoring system. For example +3 = highly favourable factor – so a potentially good opportunity for the organisation, +2 = moderately favourable factor, -1 = slightly unfavourable factor – so could represent a minor threat, -3 = highly unfavourable factor – a major threat, etc.. Which factors are most likely to have an impact on automobile manufacturers? We will return to evaluation techniques and extend this form of analysis further in Chapter 3.

Micro environment

The micro environment is closer to the organisation than the macro environment so managers can have more influence over it through competitive and collaborative moves. To understand this element of the external environment marketers need to analyse the following factors.

Markets – for example:

- Market boundaries – which products and services satisfy a particular customer need or want?
- What sub-markets already exist or are emerging?
- Who are the buyers and end users?
- How big is the market?
- How fast is it growing?
- How profitable is it?
- What are the current trends and developments?
- What is the cost structure?
- What are the key success factors for future success?

In some contexts there may be several sub-markets, each of which can be analysed using the same basic list of questions.

Industry structure and dynamics – The most common framework used to analyse an industry is the Five Forces (Porter, 1980), shown in Fig 1.2 opposite. This considers the key competitive forces at play in an industry. However, industry analysis should also include data about the size and growth of the sector, its lifecycle stage, and future changes – such as consolidation and, increasingly, existing or potential strategic partnerships. In many industries, suppliers of complementary products and services (Brandenburger and Nalebuff, 1995) are also a factor in understanding the dynamics of the sector. For example, apps are a critical part of the customer value proposition for smartphones and tablets, but the firms that produce them are not suppliers to Apple or Samsung because they have a direct and distinct relationship with the owners of the devices.

Stakeholder relationships – Both commercial and not-for-profit organisations serve a wide range of stakeholders. Some will have more influence than others but any audit of the external environment needs to take into account the views of stakeholders and the organisation's relationship with them. Identifying the stakeholders is the first step. The Seven Markets model (illustrated opposite in Fig 1.3) provides a convenient framework for listing the various groups and individuals that can have an impact and will be affected by the firm's operations.

Unlike Freidman (1970), Christopher et al (2002) acknowledge that there are important stakeholders other than the owners of the organisation (shareholders in a commercial context). The Seven Markets model links effectively to relationship marketing concepts and considers a wider range of individuals and organisations than older, classical approaches.

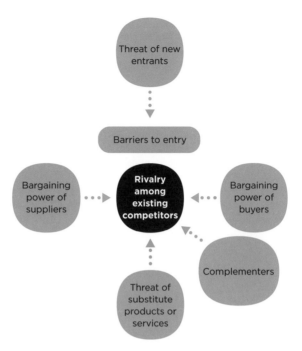

Fig 1.2 Five Forces Framework with complementers added as a sixth force. *(Sources: Porter, 1980; Brandenburger and Nalebuff, 1995)*

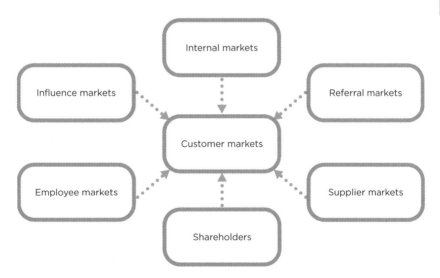

Fig 1.3 The Seven Markets model *(Source: Christopher et al 2002)*

Internal markets – Managers, employees, volunteers and other groups within the organisation can have a profound impact on the way strategy is executed (as we will see in later chapters) so marketers need to understand and manage them during each phase of the planning process.

Supplier markets – These are also much more involved in strategic planning these days, especially for firms that rely heavily on a network or eco-system of suppliers and producers of complementary products and services, are also much more involved in strategic planning these days. Toyota, Airbus and other large firms manufacturing complex products have practised a partnership approach to developing strategy for many years.

Referral markets – These can also have a significant investment in the development of an organisation's strategic marketing. In many fields business often comes from third-party referrals. Lawyers and accountants, for example, will often cross-refer clients when their own firm can't provide a particular service.

Employee markets – The channels and communities that supply potential and existing members of staff can affect the resources and capabilities of the organisation and hence its strategy (Chapters 2 and 3 will look at aspects of this further). Relationships with recruitment agencies, professional bodies such as CIM and even online discussion forums can have an impact over who the organisation is able to recruit.

Influence markets – Whether it is the media, City analysts, lenders or opinion leaders in a particular field, this group also influences the strategic planning process. For example, analysts' reports can have either a positive or negative effect on an organisation's share price or its ability to raise capital, depending on their opinion about the future direction of the organisation.

Customers – Both actual and potential customers must be at the heart of the strategic marketing planning process. We will now look at this critical group in further detail.

Aaker and McLoughlin (2010) suggest three areas of inquiry:

- Segmentation.
- Customer motivations.
- Unmet needs.

But it is also worth considering how customers purchase products and services, as well as external environmental influences that might affect customer choice (Cravens and Piercy, 2012).

Competitors – Key questions to answer here are:

- Who are our current or usual competitors?
- How intense is the level of competition?
- Can our competitors be classified into different strategic groups?
- Are they competing directly or through substitute products?
- Who are our potential competitors and what might encourage or prevent them from entering our market or industry?
- What are our competitors' objectives and strategies?
- How committed are they to our markets?
- What is their cost structure, and does this give them a competitive advantage?
- What is their market position?
- What distinctive capabilities and resources do they have?
- How have they performed (financially, market share etc) recently and in the past?

Suppliers, intermediaries and other channel members
– key questions include:

- Are suppliers' products in short supply?
- Is the supplier's product/service highly differentiated or a commodity item?
- What are the costs of switching to another supplier?
- Are there viable substitutes readily available for the supplier's product/service?
- How significant a customer is our organisation to the supplier?
- How concentrated is the supply chain – are there a few large suppliers or many small ones?
- Could we supply the products or services ourselves?
- How significant is our business to the intermediaries or channels to market?
- What has the performance of each channel or intermediary been over time?
- Could the intermediary or channel member supply the product or service we produce?

From this analysis we can determine how powerful each element of the industry supply chain is.

The core text and supplementary books all cover this aspect of external analysis in considerable detail (see 'Further reading' section at the end of the chapter) and it is worth spending time studying the relevant chapters for a more in-depth understanding of the theory and processes that underpin this activity. We will return to the tools and techniques used for external analysis in Chapter 3, where we will examine some more advanced concepts.

PROBLEMS ASSOCIATED WITH ANALYSING THE EXTERNAL ENVIRONMENT

Marketers face a number of practical issues and policy decisions as they plan how to analyse the external environment. In order to provide effective information on which to base strategic marketing decisions it is often necessary to change the way the organisation and members of staff behave. This poses a whole series of problems and challenges.

Reactive vs. proactive – Many organisations have a reactive approach to the external environment – that is, they respond to specific changes, such as new competitors, advances in technology and government regulations – as they arise. While you could argue that they are being 'responsive', such an approach can also leave an organisation vulnerable to profound changes that require it to radically alter its business model or the resources and capabilities it relies on for its competitive advantage.

A more proactive approach to the external environment involves anticipating potential changes and developing action plans in advance. However, this style of strategy requires strong research capabilities and extensive resources to support the collection and analysis of intelligence. Analysing the external environment can be a costly exercise, especially as the amount of data generated by the internet, social media and mobile has grown exponentially. Proactive strategy approaches can be difficult to justify unless there is a clear business case for the investment needed. We will look at scenario planning in Chapter 3 as an example of a tool that helps managers to anticipate future changes in their environment.

ACTIVITY 1.2

Think about the organisation you work for or one that you know well. What approach does it take to analysing its external environment – is it reactive or proactive? You may find it helpful to canvass the views of some of your colleagues or staff who work for the organisation you choose.

'Blue ocean' vs. 'red ocean' strategic thinking – When Kim and Mauborgne (2004) put forward their ideas on 'blue ocean' approaches to strategy, these were readily taken up by executives. The idea of creating a blue ocean for an organisation that will lead to between ten and 15 years of monopoly-type profits is a very compelling proposition. According to Kim and Mauborgne, remaining in an overcrowded and competitive industry (or a 'red ocean') is unlikely to lead to sustained performance. Red ocean strategic thinking is about beating the competition and exploiting existing demand. In order to do this, an organisation has to be configured to support either a low-cost or a differentiated position in the industry. Kim and Mauborgne criticise this approach (which is largely based on the works of Michael Porter) and claim that firms should instead seek uncontested market space and combine low-cost and differentiated positions to achieve this. Blue ocean strategies therefore require organisations to seek out and create new markets. Kim and Mauborgne also challenge the assumption that external analysis should focus at an industry level.

Many organisations have successfully followed a blue ocean strategy, including Canadian entertainment firm Cirque du Soleil. Others though have tried and failed to create blue oceans in their industry, as the case study below illustrates.

CASE STUDY 1.2
Blue ocean turns red for Nintendo

Nintendo's Wii console, launched in 2006, and its handheld DS gaming device, were both part of the firm's much-vaunted blue ocean strategy, which was designed to target non-gamers and expand the market for video games. Nintendo executives talked openly to the media about the blue ocean they had created and for a time it looked as if they had beaten close rivals Sony and Microsoft. Nintendo sold over 16 million units in 2007, more than double the sales of the equivalent consoles (the Xbox360 and Playstation 3) launched by each of their rivals. However, Sony and Microsoft soon produced equivalents to the Wii's motion controller and the casual gamers who were the target market for the DS began to migrate to gaming through apps on their smartphones and tablets. By 2011 Nintendo was reporting substantial losses and a significant fall in its share price.

Sources: Hollensen, S., 2013; O'Gorman. P., 2008; Thompson et al, 2013.

Risks associated with interpretation and judgement – We looked at the importance of making judgements and interpreting data from research and intelligence earlier in this chapter. However, this is not an exact science, especially in new markets or for new products. It is important to be clear about the assumptions that underpin analysis of the external environment – especially in less predictable environments. Complex and ambiguous situations can lead to biased interpretation of information and flawed judgements. Schoemaker and Day (2009) identify three traps that can lead marketers and organisations to misread their external environment:

- **Filtering** – Or selected perception. Managers tend to see what they expect to see and will filter out aspects of the external environment that don't fit their perception of the market or industry.

- **Distorted inference** – Managers interpret the evidence in a way that sustains their beliefs or biases.
- **Bolstering** – Managers search for additional evidence in support of their views.

Barriers to effective marketing planning – As we have seen above, effective analysis of the external environment is complex, time consuming and costly, and McDonald and Wilson (2016) warn that implementing a formalised marketing planning system is far from straightforward. They highlight a number of key barriers to effective marketing planning:

- **Weak or non-existent support from the top**, which can result in senior managers ignoring requests for information and data needed for planning, or providing only partial information.
- **Lack of an implementation plan** for introducing the new system. As with any organisational change, you need a robust plan, including enlisting the help of internal marketing to sell the new processes and procedures to key players.
- **Lack of line management support**, especially if the planning system requires more work but is not effectively resourced.
- **Overuse of jargon and terminology** by planners. Not everyone in the business has the same level of knowledge about business theory and planning tools, so it's is important to interpret these for the intended audience.
- **Lack of narrative**. The process becomes too focused on numbers, trends and forecasts without giving a supporting narrative about the underlying causes of change.
- **Over-analysis and paralysis by analysis**. Much of the data collected is too detailed or not used in the planning process.
- **A once-a-year activity**. This can mean developments and changes in the external environment are not acted on quickly enough, especially in dynamic and volatile markets.
- **Lack of integration** between strategy and operations planning and various corporate and functional planning systems,
- **Delegating the whole process to the planners**, who may be highly qualified but lack experience.

Data gathering and analysis: skills and challenges – The growth of mobile, the internet and social media has had a profound effect on the skills needed to analyse the external environment. We started this chapter by considering some of the skills marketers need to analyse markets. Other challenges include understanding and managing the ethical issues associated with using the mass of data organisations collect and hold on their customers.

QUICK QUIZ – CHECK YOUR KNOWLEDGE

Questions

1. What are the five factors that underpin a market orientation?
2. Why did Nintendo's attempt to create a blue ocean fail?
3. What is the difference between an organisation's macro and micro environments?
4. What is the difference between a proactive and reactive approach to external analysis?

Answers

1. Focus on long-term profits, strategic rather than tactical approach, customer orientation, competitor orientation, inter-functional co-ordination within the organisation.
2. The new market space they created lacked sufficient barriers to entry so their rivals and a range of new entrants and producers of substitutes were able to move rapidly into the market.
3. The macro environment is the broad environment covering factors that affect all organisations and over which they have little or no influence. The micro environment is closer and comprises industry, market and value-chain members.
4. Proactive approaches mean anticipating issues and having plans in place to mitigate them, whereas reactive means responding to changes as and when they happen.

FURTHER READING

Books

Core text:

Hooley, G., Nicoulaud, B., Piercy, N. and Rudd, J. (2017) *Marketing strategy and competitive positioning*. 6th edition. Harlow, FT Prentice Hall. Chapters 1-5.

Supplementary texts:

Aaker, D. and McLouglin, D. (2010) *Strategic market management: global perspectives*. Chichester, John Wiley. Chapters 1-5.

Cravens, D.W. and Piercy, N. (2012) *Strategic marketing*. 10th edition. US, McGraw-Hill. Chapters 1 and 2.

McDonald, M. and Wilson, H. (2016) *Marketing plans: how to prepare them, how to profit from them*. Chichester, John Wiley.

References

Anon (2013a) Markets and makers: running harder. *The Economist*, 20 April 2013, Special Report: Cars, pp4-7.

Anon (2013b) General Electric Motors. *The Economist*, 20 April 2013, Special Report: Cars, p6.

Anon (2013c) The great power train race. *The Economist*, 20 April 2013, Special Report: Cars, pp9-11.

Anon (2013d) Green wheels. *The Economist*, 20 April 2013, Special Report: Cars, p9.

Anon (2013e) Driverless cars: look no hands. *The Economist*, 20 April 2013, Special Report: Cars, pp12-14.

BBC (2013) Lego becomes world's second-biggest toy maker. *BBC News online*, 5 September. http://www.bbc.co.uk/news/business-23968860 [accessed July 2014]

BBC News (2010) European car sales see 9.2% fall. *BBC News online*, 15 October. http://www.bbc.co.uk/news/business-11549448 [accessed July 2014]

BMI (2012) *Emerging Europe automotive insight*, Issue 73, Business Monitor International.

Brandenburger, A. and Nalebuff, B. (1995) The right game. *Harvard Business Review*, July-August, pp57-71.

Christopher, M., Payne, A. and Ballantyne, D. (2002) *Relationship marketing: creating stakeholder value.* Oxford, Butterworth-Heinemann.

First Research (2013) *Industry profile, automobile manufacturing*, First Research, Boston.

Forth A. (2013a) *Electric vehicles intelligence service*, Aroq/Just-Auto.

Forth, A. (2013b) *Automotive markets intelligence service.* Aroq/Just-Auto.

Freeman, R. (1984) *Strategic management: a stakeholder approach*, London, Harper-Collins.

Gott, P. (2008) Is mobility as we know it sustainable? EET-2008 European Ele-Drive Conference Case Study: *The future of the motor industry*, International Advanced Mobility *Forum* Geneva, Switzerland, 11-13 March 2008.

Greene, J. (2010) How LEGO revived its brand. *Bloomberg BusinessWeek*, 23 July. http://www.businessweek.com/innovate/content/jul2010/id20100722_781838.htm [accessed July 2014]

Hollensen, S. (2013) The blue ocean that disappeared – the case of Nintendo Wii. *Journal of Business Strategy*, Vol24(5), pp25-35.

Kekic, L. and Nichols, A. (2013) *Industry report: automotive: Russia*, London, Economist Intelligence Unit, January.

LEGO (2006-2014) Various annual reports.

License Europe (2006) Rebuilding LEGO. *License Europe*, November–December, pp24-29.

Mintzberg, H. and Waters, J. (1985) Of strategies, deliberate and emergent. *Strategic Management Journal*, Vol6(3) pp257-272.

O'Gorman. P. (2008) Wii: creating a blue ocean the Nintendo way. *Palermo Business Review*, No.2, pp97-108.

Porter, M. (1980) *Competitive strategy: techniques for analyzing industries and competitors,* New York, Free Press.

Robertson, D. and Hjuler, P. (2009) Innovating a turnaround at LEGO. *Harvard Business Review*, September, pp20-21.

Rust, R., Moorman, C., and Bhalla, G. (2010) Re-thinking marketing. *Harvard Business Review*, January-February, p96.

Schoemaker, P. and Day, G. (2009) How to make sense of weak signals. *MIT Sloan Management Review*, Vol50(3), pp81-89.

Schumpeter (2012) The driverless road ahead. *The Economist*, 20 October 2012, p68.

Thompson, A.A., Peteraf, M., Gamble, J.E., Strickland, A.J. III., Janes, A. and Sutton, C. (2013) *Crafting and executing strategy, the quest for competitive advantage: concepts and cases*, Maidenhead, McGraw-Hill.

Wallop, H. (2012) LEGO sees its profits continue to stack up. *Daily Telegraph*, Business, 2 March, p3.

Weiners, B. (2011) Lego is for girls. *Bloomberg BusinessWeek,* 14 December. http://www.businessweek.com/magazine/lego-is-for-girls-12142011.html [accessed July 2014]

2.
SITUATION ANALYSIS: THE CURRENT AND FUTURE INTERNAL ENVIRONMENT

OUTLINE

This chapter will help you tounderstand how to analyse an organisation's current and future internal environment. At the end of this chapter you will be able to:

- Understand how resources, assets, competencies and capabilities support the achievement of competitive advantage by creating and delivering value.
- Explain how to use a range of financial measures to determine the relative performance of an organisation.
- Recognise how limited organisational resources can act as a barrier to achieving a sustainable competitive advantage.

DEFINITIONS

Resources – The portfolio of assets owned or managed by an organisation.

Capabilities – The ways in which an organisation uses its assets and resources or realises their potential.

Core competencies – Activities carried out skilfully and efficiently and that are central to an organisation's success.

Dynamic capabilities – "An organisation's ability to renew and recreate its strategic capabilities to meet the needs of changing environments." (Teece *et al*, 1997)

Brand equity – "A set of assets and liabilities linked to a brand name and symbol that add to or subtract from the value provided by a product or service to a firm or that firm's customers." (Aaker, 1991)

Value chain – The primary activities that create value for the customer and the support activities that enable and enhance them.

RESOURCES, COMPETENCIES AND CAPABILITIES

As we saw in Chapter 1, marketers have to respond to and anticipate changes in the external environment and the needs of the market. They also need to understand their organisation's internal environment. One of the key theories that has developed in recent years to help explain the way factors within the organisation contribute to competitive advantage is the **Resource Based View (RBV)**. RBV stems from economic theory in the late 1950s (Penrose, 1959) that looked at the firm as a bundle of resources developed over time, which, in turn, gives certain organisations a competitive advantage over others. More recently these ideas have been codified through an extensive body of literature (and some of the key articles are covered in the 'Further reading' section at the end of the chapter).

What do we mean by **resources**? Some theorists refer to all the strengths and weaknesses of an organisation as resources (Wernerfelt, 1984; Barney, 1991). However, in order to highlight the distinction between resources and capabilities, Day's (1994) approach is a useful one to begin with. Day classified resources as both tangible and intangible assets – so these might be physical resources, such as factories, plant and machinery, or financial assets, such as cash and access to capital, but they could also be less concrete assets, such as brands, knowledge, patents and trademarks. They are all controlled or owned by the organisation.

What do we mean by **capabilities**? These are the skills and abilities that allow the organisation to exploit the resources or assets it has built up over time. They are what it is good at. Capabilities could be single tasks, like greeting guests in a hotel, functional abilities, such as brand management, or integrated across a range of functions, such as new product development or acquiring and integrating other organisations.

ACTIVITY 2.1

Think about a car journey from one city to another. What resources (assets) and what capabilities (skills and abilities) would you need to complete this journey?

Identifying resources and capabilities

Using different categories to list an organisation's resources and capabilities is an important part of internal analysis since it ensures managers don't overlook or miss any competitively important strengths or critical weaknesses.

Thompson *et al* (2013) provide a framework with four categories of tangible resource and four types of intangible resource.

Tangible resources
- **Physical resources** – Facilities, property and natural resources, for example (either owned or with rights of access or control). So things like land, factories, retail outlets, equipment, distribution and other logistics assets, minerals and oil.
- **Financial resources** – Working capital, cash, borrowing capacity and marketable securities, for example.
- **Technological assets** – These include legally enforceable assets such as ownership of copyrights and patents, along with things like trade secrets and operational assets such as production technology and technical processes.
- **Organisational resources** – Systems-based assets such as planning, co-ordination and control systems, and the design of the organisation's management and marketing information systems and databases – especially those used to support strategic decision making.

Intangible resources
- **Human assets and intellectual capital** – This is more than just the number of staff employed; it is the experience, knowledge, innovation, creativity and learning they bring to the organisation and the knowhow of key employees and teams.
- **Brands, image and reputational assets** – These are key customer and stakeholder-based assets, from trademarks and brand names, through customer loyalty to reputation in the marketplace. For some organisations country of origin can play a part, as can unique products and services and franchised brands.
- **Relationships** – These include distribution and dealer networks and the level of control an organisation has over them; supply chain partnerships; and more diverse strategic alliances and joint ventures for entering new markets and/or developing new products and services or providing complementary products and services.
- **Organisational culture and incentive systems** – These cover the beliefs, assumptions and values of the organisation and the norms by which employees behave, as well as the levels of motivation and innovation within the firm.

As we have seen, resources are linked to capabilities, so one way to identify an organisation's skills and abilities is to start by looking at the assets it controls and draw conclusions from this about its capabilities. For example, luxury goods company LVMH controls a range of premium brands, from fashion and leather goods manufacturer Louis Vuitton, to Champagne maker Moët and Chandon. From this we can conclude that the firm has the capability of luxury brand management. Looking at the number of brands the firm owns we can extend this and identify another capability as managing a portfolio of luxury brands.

Another way to identify capabilities is to take a more functional approach. Grant (2010) provides a useful hierarchy of capabilities that ensures managers also include capabilities that are cross functional and involve several parts of the organisation. (Fig 2.1 opposite demonstrates this framework applied to the hotel industry.)

An organisation's value chain (Porter 1985) is another way of categorising capabilities and the manner in which they interact to produce value for the customer and profit or surplus for the organisation. We will look at this tool further below.

REAL LIFE 2.1
Accor's capabilities

Global France-based hotel chain Accor has over 4,200 hotels and 145,000 employees in 90 countries. With 14 hotel brands the group covers a wide range of sectors. Although Accor's current strengths lie in economy and no-frills brands such as Ibis, hotelF1 and Motel6 its roots were in mid-market chains like Novotel and Mercure. Accor has also demonstrated that it can create and manage upscale brands such as Pullman and MGallery, as well as succeed with luxury established brands including Sofitel.

The company embarked on its international growth path in 1973 when it opened a hotel in Warsaw, Poland, its first hotel outside France. In 1974 it launched a new two-star hotel brand, the Ibis, in Bordeaux. In addition to organic growth Accor has a history of acquiring other hotel businesses. It bought the rival three-star operator Mercure in 1975 and the four-star deluxe hotel chain Sofitel in 1980. More recently Accor spearheaded its expansion in Australia and New Zealand with the acquisition of the hotel management firm Mirvac in 2011. Accor has continued to develop new hotel brands and launched Pullman and a new chain of economy hotels, All Seasons, in 2007.

The group has always sold under-performing hotels, thereby releasing capital to support its expansion. However, most of the capital for its recent expansion in Asia Pacific was raised by an 'asset light' approach, which involved the sale and leaseback of the group's owned hotel properties in Europe and North America.

Accor has discovered the many advantages in partnerships both inside and outside of the industry. In 2009 it consolidated its position as a provider of pre-pay services through a joint venture with MasterCard in Europe. The move to a combination of asset-light and franchise models in Europe and part of Asia-Pacific has given the firm more alliances with property owners and franchisees.

Many of Accor's biggest successes are the result of taking a non-traditional approach. It has always innovated, both in terms of the hotel brands it has developed and the processes that underpin its operations. For example, in the 1960s and 1970s it was one of the first companies to build airport hotels and to standardise the front of house and other functions, such as dining and restaurant services. Technological advances, including electronic reservation and other computerised systems, have also had a profound effect on its business model. More recently the group has invested in fitness rooms, takeaway services for guests and environmental policies to maintain its competitive position in the marketplace.

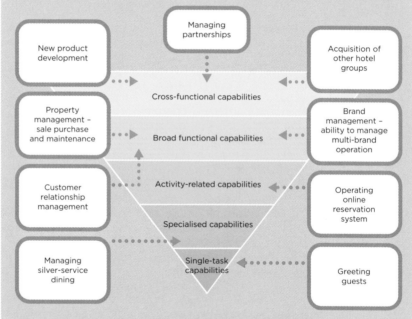

Fig 2.1 Grant's hierarchy framework applied to a selection of Accor's capabilities (*Sources: Adapted from Grant, 2010; and Janes, 2013*)

Competitive advantage

Having identified all the resources and capabilities in the organisation, you have to assess each one in terms of its contribution to the firm's competitive advantage (or lack of it). Jay Barney (1991) proposed four tests – valuable, rare, inimitable and non-substitutable – that a resource or capability must pass in order to support and sustain a competitive advantage. These tests are often referred to by the acronym **VRIN**.

A resource or capability which can support a competitive advantage should be:

Valuable – The resource or capability allows the organisation to exploit opportunities or mitigate threats and is relevant to its strategy. It should be able to enhance the organisation's business model through making either the customer value proposition or the operating model more effective or efficient.

Rare – Only a few organisations in the sector or market control the resource or have the capability. In the global hotel sector, brands such as Novotel, Holiday Inn and Crowne Plaza are valuable, but as all the major players, including Accor, Hilton and Marriott, have a portfolio of brands, this does not constitute a 'rare' resource.

In order to sustain competitive advantage over a longer period of time the resource or capability needs to pass two additional tests:

Inimitable – It's hard to copy. A number of factors can make a resource or capability inimitable, for example:

- It may be socially complex or difficult to analyse ('causally ambiguous'). For example, animated film studio Pixar's creativity and innovation capabilities are difficult for other firms to copy because they are embedded in the organisation's culture. Disney bought the company because it saw it as a less expensive way of acquiring these capabilities than trying to develop them in-house.
- It may have been built up over many years. For example, established food and drink brands such as Coca-Cola and Heinz have invested in brand building over many years, and the cost of achieving the same level of recognition and loyalty in a short time would be prohibitively expensive for most organisations. Similarly, organisations that have owned city centre property or prime retail sites for many years will have a significant advantage over newer rivals.

Non-substitutable – If there are no equivalent alternatives then the resource or capability would pass this final test. However, it can be difficult to know just what customers would perceive as an acceptable substitute.

More recent studies (Barney and Hesterly, 2011) have suggested one further test:

Does the organisation exploit the resource or capability? – Managers need to configure their organisation in order to make most effective use of the key resources and capabilities identified in their internal audit. This might be the way the organisation is structured, its policies and systems or its culture. This has been captured as the VRIO framework. The 'V' and 'R' being the same as in VRIN, then the 'I' referred to as 'costly to imitate' and the 'O' being 'organised'.

39

CASE STUDY 2.1

What underpins the 'fast fashion' phenomenon?

It took 25 years to turn a small Spanish dressing-gown manufacturing company into the toast of the retail fashion industry. Commentators and competitors alike have found much to praise in Inditex's approach to making and selling clothing, which involves creating affordable catwalk-inspired products within days of them appearing at fashion shows. It is a model that many high street retailers are striving to emulate.

Inditex, the parent company of the Zara, Pull & Bear, Massimo Dutti, Bershka, Stradivarius and Oysho brands, is still mostly owned by the Ortega family despite going public in 2001. And it has always taken a long-term approach to business. A unique approach to supply chain management is at the heart of the firm's success. Between 2000 and 2010 most clothing retailers outsourced production to Asia, and it typically took between six and nine months to get clothes from design to shop. Inditex has pared this down to between two and five weeks. It does have operations in North Africa and some parts of Asia, but it manufactures about half its clothes in north-west Spain. An important element in its approach is the co-location of designers, factories and distribution centres at its headquarters site in La Coruna. The group employs over 128,000 professionals in 87 countries representing 150 nationalities. The close working relationships between different teams – from those in the retail outlets to those in corporate areas such as finance and human resources – is seen internally as an important part of the company's customer orientation.

Inditex also takes what might appear to be a counter-intuitive approach to production. Rather than seeking economies of scale through predicting future fashion trends and producing in mass to meet demand, it makes its clothes in deliberately small batches in order to create a scarcity value. When the company first opened stores in the UK shop assistants had to explain to customers used to waiting for end of season sales that once stock sold out it was usually gone for good. New lines and products are delivered to stores twice a week. One of the ways that Inditex out-performs competitors is in the low number of items that end up in sales and are therefore sold at a discount. Shop staff at the firm's 6,000 retail outlets are encouraged to provide feedback to headquarters on the latest trends they observe and what customers are requesting in store. Inditex regards itself as a company that innovates continuously, and this extends to every aspect of the business, from the fashion items to the environment in its stores.

The other leading firms in the fast-fashion end of retail, such as Gap, Uniqlo and H&M, have enjoyed substantial growth and their business models have proved successful around the globe. But increasing pressure on margins, volatile commodity prices and environmental concerns could spell the end of the fast-fashion phenomenon. Gap and H&M are more vulnerable to such changes than Inditex because of their outsourced manufacturing model. H&M has many suppliers in Asia and has seen costs rise as a result of increasing wage levels in China. On the other hand, H&M has benefited from strong links with designers such as Karl Lagerfeld and Stella McCartney, as well as celebrities like Madonna. All the leading firms in this sector have a strong portfolio of brands – Gap, for example, owns Banana Republic, Old Navy and Piperlime.

Sources: BBC, 2004; The Economist, 2009; Inditex, 2014; Foroohar, 2006; Datamonitor, 2014; Gap Inc., 2014.

ACTIVITY 2.2
Using the resource and capability categories listed above and the VRIN/O framework, identify Inditex's resources and capabilities and decide which of them support and sustain its competitive advantage over its competitors.

Core competencies
Other experts have proposed alternative ways of determining whether bundles of resources and capabilities can give an organisation an advantage over its rivals. Prahalad and Hamel (1990) put forward the idea of core competencies as a way of explaining competitive advantage and they focused particularly on knowledge-based assets and capabilities. For a competency to be considered core it has to pass three tests:

1. It needs to provide the organisation with the possibility of accessing a wide range of markets.
2. It needs to underpin and add significantly to the customer value of a product or service.
3. It must be difficult for rivals to imitate.

Dynamic capabilities
In the previous chapter we looked at how the external environment of an organisation can be characterised according to how quickly and

how radically it is changing. Some capabilities can help organisations adapt to changes in their environment. These give an organisation the ability to change its resource base and, in some cases, its capabilities. Recent research (Ambrosini *et al*, 2009) identified three types of 'dynamic capabilities':

- **Incremental capabilities** – Allow the organisation to adapt its resource base on an incremental basis. They are present even in organisations operating in stable environments. In practical terms, they tend to be part of a continuous improvement process – improving packaging or waste management, for example.
- **Renewing capabilities** – Help the firm to renew its resource base and are needed in dynamic environments where the organisation's competitive advantage can be eroded. Examples include developing brand extensions (as Virgin does) or extending a corporate brand into adjacent markets (like Cisco).
- **Regenerative capabilities** – Are needed in the most uncertain and volatile environments and enable the organisation to change its entire business model and the dynamic capabilities that it has previously relied on.

These strengths allow the organisation to create new assets and capabilities and encourage learning and experimentation. For example, the ability to generate insights from customer research can help a firm to develop new customer resources, such as brands.

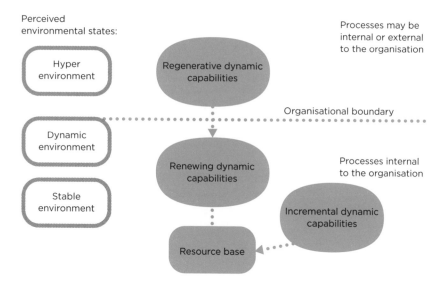

Figure 2.2 Levels of dynamic capability *(Source: Ambrosini et al, 2009)*

CASE STUDY 2.2
Bookshops reinvent themselves

The bookselling trade is facing discontinuous change due to dramatic shifts in the way people read books. In the UK and US many independent book shops and even some of the larger chain stores have failed because technology has made online buying and selling of books the norm and allowed customers access to a huge range of digitised books through e-readers.

Internet giant Amazon has demonstrated its dynamic capabilities through its move from online bookstore to selling a wide range of merchandise, developing tablet devices such as the Kindle and becoming a publisher (a strategy known as 'backward integrating').

But the surviving bookshops are fighting back and demonstrating their own dynamic capabilities by embracing many of the changes in their marketplace and changing the way they operate. US book chain Barnes and Noble, for example, has launched its own e-reader, the Nook, and has moved into digital publishing. Other players, such as UK retailer Waterstones, have used their knowledge of customers to create a different customer experience in their stores. Many Waterstones branches now include coffee shops and the firm has partnered with the University of Derby to create the first professional qualification in bookselling in order to ensure their shop staff can provide expert advice to customers. This personal approach is in stark contrast to the user reviews and algorithm-driven recommendations on Amazon.com.

All the survivors in the bookselling market have demonstrated both incremental and renewing dynamic capabilities. Amazon has extended its business model into many more areas of retail than books – evidence of a renewing dynamic capability. Barnes and Noble has used its knowledge of publishing to backward integrate and take the role of the publisher. And Waterstones' incremental capabilities are evident in the way it has changed the customer experience with the addition of the coffee shops and so on. The big question for the 'bricks and mortar' retailers though is whether they can change their business model in a regenerative manner.

Sources: Campbell, 2013; Key Note, 2013; Flood, 2013; Anthony, 2012; Griffiths, 2012; Rankin, 2013.

Culture, leadership and management

In the Inditex case study we saw how the culture of the organisation and the leadership of the Ortega family are important factors in the company's success. Culture is one of the hardest resources to analyse because of its complex and intangible nature and the fact that it often develops organically. But strong cultures have a profound impact on management's ability to implement a strategy so marketers need to understand this aspect of the internal environment in more depth.

Schein (2010) identified three key elements to an organisation's culture:

- **Artefacts and behaviours** – These are the most observable elements of culture and include everything from the way people dress at work and behave with fellow workers, customers, suppliers and other stakeholders, to the architecture, furniture and office layout and even the stories that are told to new recruits.
- **Espoused values** – These are often stated alongside the mission or vision for the organisation, and are part of its official identity.

- **Basic assumptions** – These are the taken-for-granted paradigms and beliefs that underpin the first two aspects of culture. Most employees aren't consciously aware of these elements as they are the most deeply embedded – which also makes them the most difficult to research.

Changing an organisation's culture – especially when it is preventing new strategies being implemented – is one of the toughest leadership tasks managers face.

Innovation auditing

As we have seen in some of the case studies above, successful organisations are good at innovation. They can create new products and services or change the way they deliver those goods and benefits. In order to innovate effectively, organisations need to be able to tap into the creativity of their workforce, or encourage staff to be more creative. Organisations need certain resources and capabilities in order to be innovative, and an innovation audit helps them to identify which of these they already have and where they need to improve.

There are four components to a traditional innovation audit.

The **organisational climate** – This is often determined through the use of a staff survey. Innovation specialists and academics (Burnside, 1991; Isaksen and Ekvall, 2010) have developed a number of templates but broadly speaking they all measure similar attributes:

- **Challenge/involvement** – The higher the challenge and involvement the better the levels of engagement.
- **Freedom** – The amount of independence or autonomy employees are given.
- **Trust/openness** – Strong open relationships within the organisation can foster greater innovation and build teams that are committed to each other and are willing to help fellow employees.
- **Idea time** – The amount of time set aside for employees to work on new ideas. Lack of time can be a constraint on innovation.
- **Playfulness/humour** – Indicates of a relaxed atmosphere and spontaneity.
- **Conflict** – Some creative tension is required for successful innovation but when this becomes personal or emotional and leads to political behaviour it can undermine innovation.
- **Idea support** – In the form of resources and infrastructure, but also ensuring that ideas are given a fair hearing.
- **Debate** – The positive side of conflict. Disagreements are managed and encouraged with different viewpoints given a fair hearing.
- **Risk taking** – Is encouraged, and the organisation tolerates ambiguity and uncertainty about outcomes. Over-evaluation and too much measurement are not conducive to innovation.

- **Recognition** – Reward and incentive systems should recognise creativity.

Specific **measures of innovation performance** – These may include analysis of the number of new products or services launched over a period of time, the percentage of sales generated by new products and the success rate of new products. But this has to be balanced with the ability to take risks and act autonomously – as shown above – and the nature of the business in which the organisation is engaged.

Supporting policies and systems – Some clues to this element of the audit will come from researching the creative climate, but there will also be a range of tacit and explicit material – from schemes that encourage suggestions and incentivise incremental changes (such as through 'kaizen'-type improvements to processes), to time built into the working day for all employees to work on their own projects. Google, for instance, allows technical staff to spend 20% of their time working on projects of their own choosing, and Gmail, Adsense and Google News were all developed through this process (Iyer and Davenport, 2008).

Senior management team's cognitive styles – A diverse group of senior managers with different cognitive styles will have an impact on the level of creativity and innovation in the organisation. For example, if most of the senior management team are intuitive the organisation will tend to be very future oriented but may not be able to exploit the full business potential of inventions. (Hurst *et al*, 1989) Entrepreneurial traits are also increasingly valued even in large multinational and public sector organisations. The cognitive styles of managers can be determined in a number of ways, but a common tool is the Myers Briggs Type Indicator (MBTI) which uses a combination of four styles:

- **Intuitive** – Ingenious and integrative individuals who focus on patterns and ideas and commonly use symbols and metaphors.
- **Sensing** – Practical and adaptable managers who tend to be driven by events and activities and are very action oriented.
- **Thinking** – Pragmatists who take an objective and logical approach to the workplace and favour regulations and policies.
- **Feeling** – Insightful and empathetic individuals who focus on people and values.

MBTI then uses a scoring system based on a personal questionnaire to allocate people to one of 16 different personality types.

As innovation is becoming much more open and often involves multiple strategic partners and networks of organisations and individuals, current and future audits also need to take into account the partnerships and platforms that support this activity.

Risks of innovation

Managers also need to be aware that innovation and new product development can be risky. Innovation requires a substantial investment of time and other resources and there is no guarantee of success. Risks include investing too many financial resources in the wrong projects, developing new products and services that don't create sufficient market demand and, at an operational level, failing to meet launch dates and cost and quality targets for the project. There is also the risk that the innovation will deliver only a short-lived competitive advantage (as we saw in the Nintendo case study in Chapter 1) because rivals can easily copy the new product or service and, as second movers, learn from first movers' mistakes.

Brand equity analysis

A particularly significant resource for marketers is the brand or brands that their organisation owns. As a key asset in generating customer value the brand is critical to any internal analysis on which to base the organisation's marketing strategy. Brands are now frequently listed in the intangible assets of a company's balance sheet, and companies have to attach a value to them if they have acquired them (though not, currently, if they have developed them internally). Trading in brands started in earnest in the 1980s and a whole industry has grown up around brand valuation – a subject that we will cover in Chapter 3.

According to Aaker (1995) determining a brand's equity requires analysis of the awareness of the brand name, the level of brand loyalty and perceived quality among customers and the various elements that make up the brand's identity. The stronger each of these aspects of the brand is, the more valuable the brand asset.

Value chain

Managers can often become very focused on their own organisation's resources and capabilities when conducting an internal analysis. But as we've seen in some of the examples and activities above, you also have to compare your own assets and abilities with those of rivals in order to determine how competitively valuable they are. Porter (1985) developed a generic **value-chain framework** to help managers analyse their organisation's activities and those of their competitors. The tool has five primary elements:

- **Inbound logistics** – Activities that cover the flow of products or raw materials into the organisation.
- **Operations** – Processes that change these inputs into products the company then sells on.
- **Outbound logistics** – Distribution activities to buyers.
- **Marketing and sales** – Activities including market research, promotion, sales force efforts and support for distributors and dealers.
- **Service** – After-sales activities such as installation and supply of spare parts.

In addition the tool has three or four supporting activities:

- **R&D/technology development** – Activities that underpin new product and process development.
- **Human resources management** – Activities such as recruitment, hiring, training and developing staff, as well as incentive schemes.
- **Infrastructure/general administration** – Underpinning systems and assets connected to accounting and finance, legal, procurement (some value-chain frameworks have this as a separate element) and other corporate functions.

REAL LIFE 2.3

How Aldi uses the value chain to underpin its business model

German supermarket firm Aldi has developed a no-frills approach to retailing that has helped it to expand beyond its traditional base in Germany to other parts of Europe, including the United Kingdom, Poland and the Czech Republic. Almost every element of the firm's value chain is geared to reducing the cost of its operations. (See Fig 2.3 below.)

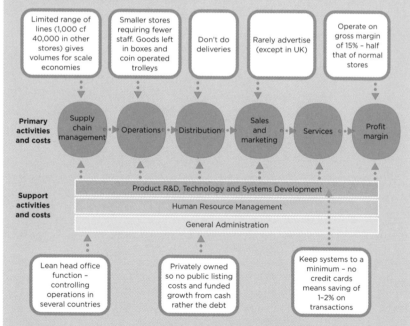

Fig 2.3 How Aldi reduces operating costs throughout its value chain
(Sources: Adapted from Porter, 1985; and Thompson et al, 2013)

Analysing an organisation's value chain and those of its competitors can help managers understand the cost structures of each organisation and how they can generate competitive advantage through operating differently or more efficiently than their rivals.

In Chapter 3 we will look at how you could use some of these ideas to construct practical frameworks to determine the value of your organisation's resources and capabilities.

MEASURING MARKETING PERFORMANCE

Financial resources are a key tangible asset for organisations because they allow it to invest in other resources and capabilities. They are also one of the most widely used indicators for measuring the performance of an organisation's strategy. When thinking about an organisation's strengths and weaknesses marketers can gain useful insights by looking at a range of financial measures over time and in comparison with close competitors. Below are some of the most common ratios and measures used to assess financial and marketing performance.

Sales – The turnover of the organisation or the income it generates from producing goods or delivering services. As a raw measure of success, sales trends can be a useful indicator of growth, but marketers should remember the old maxim: turnover is vanity, profit is sanity.

Market share – In its most basic form is determined by dividing the sales generated by the organisation by the sales of all the organisations supplying the particular market being analysed.

Profits – The ratios that show the return the organisation has made on the assets it has invested. They are important for shareholders and other investors in the organisation. The main ratios used are as follows:

- **Net profit margin** shows profits per currency unit of sales. To be a strength this should be higher than the industry average or that of close competitors, and the trend should be upwards.

$$\frac{\text{Net profit (profit after tax)}}{\text{Sales (revenues)}}$$

- **Return on Capital Employed (ROCE)** shows how well the organisation is using the capital invested in its operations. You can compare the rate with the interest the capital might have gained if it had been invested elsewhere (in a bank deposit account or in government bonds, for example). As with the net profit margin, the trend should be upwards and the figure higher than that of alternatives and competitors and industry rivals.

$$\text{ROCE} = \frac{\text{Profit before taxation}}{\text{Capital employed}}$$
$$\text{(fixed or non-current assets + net current assets)}$$

- **Liquidity** – ratios that show how solvent the organisation is. In other words, does it have enough cash to meet the payments due for its current liabilities? The most commonly used measure is the **current ratio**:

$$\text{Current ratio} = \frac{\text{Current assets}}{\text{Current liabilities}}$$

This shows an organisation's ability to pay its current liabilities with current assets (that is, assets that can be converted to cash in the short term). The ratio should be 1.0 or higher and ratios of 2.0 or better indicate a very healthy position. However, this does depend on the industry or sector in which the organisation operates. Industries where organisations hold a lot of stock (or inventory) – such as manufacturing – should have higher current ratios than those with little or no stock – such as a consultancy.

Because stock (inventory) can distort the current ratio, some analysts prefer to use a different measure for liquidity – the acid test ratio:

$$\text{Acid test ratio} = \frac{\text{Current assets} - \text{stocks}}{\text{Current liabilities}}$$

This takes account of the fact that some current assets are hard to convert into cash quickly, especially those with a low stock turnover like construction companies or firms that manufacture capital equipment. For these organisations an acid test ratio of at least 1.0 would indicate acceptable liquidity. Organisations with high stock turnover, such as supermarkets or FMCG manufacturers, might have a ratio of 0.8 and have a healthy cash flow.

- **Inventory (stock) turnover** – is a measure of asset utilisation – in other words, how efficiently the organisation is managing different aspects of its business (such as stock or inventory).

$$\text{Inventory turnover} = \frac{\text{Cost of sales}}{\text{Inventory (stock)}}$$

This ratio gives the number of times stock is completely sold and replaced each year – so the higher the figure the better.

Another way of looking at this is through **'days of inventory'**, which measures how efficiently stock is being managed. The formula is as follows:

$$\text{Days of inventory} = \frac{\text{Inventory}}{\text{Cost of sales}/365}$$

In this case the lower the number of days, the more efficiently the stock is being managed. However, this will vary depending on the type of business the organisation is engaged in. For example, a company making perishable products would need to have a much lower figure for days of inventory than a firm making consumer durables or capital equipment. As stated above, many of these figures yield more information about an organisation if they are compared over time so that trends can be determined, or if they are compared with competitors' performance or industry averages.

ACTIVITY 2.3

Below is a simplified profit and loss account and balance sheet for a company manufacturing and selling microscopy consumables.

Short accounts for Lion Components

Profit and loss accounts for the years ended 31 December 2012 and 31 December 2013

$million	2012		2013	
Sales		960		1,020
Cost of sales				
Materials	300		320	
Labour	160		162	
Distribution	130		133	
Depreciation/amortisation	90		90	
Promotion	120		130	
Plant overheads	80		80	
		(880)		(915)
Gross profit		**80**		**105**
Administration expenses				
Labour	26		36	
Loan interest	41		51	
Other expenses	3		3	
		(70)		(90)
Profit before taxation		**10**		**15**
Tax (20%)		(2)		(3)
Net profit		**8**		**12**
Dividend		(0)		(0)
Retained earnings		**8**		**12**

Balance sheet at 31 December 2013

$million		
Non-current assets		
Intangible assets	400	
Property, plant and machinery	680	
Less accumulated depreciation/amortisation	(300)	
		780
Current assets		
Stock	230	
Debtors	304	
Cash	76	
	610	
Current liabilities		
Creditors	483	
Tax	2	
Dividend payable	0	
	485	
Net current assets		125
Long-term debt		(460)
Net assets		**445**
Shareholders' interest		
437,000,000 ordinary shares authorised, issued and fully paid at $1	437	
Retained profit	8	
Equity		**445**

Using the formulas above, calculate the profit, liquidity and stock turnover figures for 2013. What do they tell you about the company? Calculate the net profit margin for 2012. How does this compare with the figure for 2013?

2.3

LIMITATIONS TO RESOURCES AS A SOURCE OF COMPETITIVE ADVANTAGE

The resource-based view is not without its critics, and the fact that even successful well-resourced organisations still fail in the face of disruptive changes in their environment has led experts to research why this occurs.

Core rigidities – Earlier we saw how important core capabilities are in differentiating an organisation from its rivals and in supporting sustained competitive advantage. But research by Leonard-Barton (1992) also showed that these same capabilities can make it difficult for organisations to innovate successfully. She termed them 'core rigidities' and demonstrated through a series of case studies how these can impede the development of new products, services and processes, leaving an organisation vulnerable to changes in its external environment.

Sticky resources – Ghemawat and del Sol (1998) coined the term 'sticky' resources to describe firm-specific assets that it is difficult or expensive to separate from the organisation that owns or controls them. These resources are worth more to this organisation than they are to any other. Investment in promoting a brand name over time would be an example of an activity producing a sticky resource. Because of the sunk costs associated with this type of resource and the fact that organisations may have built their strategy around them, they are usually reluctant to dispose of them. But this can reduce an organisation's ability to adapt to major shifts in its external environment. So, rather like core rigidities, the source of an organisation's past success can cause problems in its present and future.

QUICK QUIZ – CHECK YOUR KNOWLEDGE

Questions
1. What is the difference between resources and capabilities?
2. What are the four types of intangible assets?
3. Why is it risky for managers to identify capabilities based on the functions within the business?
4. How can marketers identify resources and capabilities that will sustain their organisation's competitive advantage?
5. According to Schein, what are the three main elements of an organisation's culture?
6. Name two aspects of an organisation's climate that can limit its creativity and ability to innovative if they are not managed effectively.
7. What do liquidity ratios such as the 'current' and 'acid test' measures show?
8. Why do core rigidities and sticky resources cause problems for organisations in dynamic environments?

Answers

1. A resource is an asset owned or controlled by the company. A capability is an ability or skills applied to utilise the resource or asset. One way to remember the difference is through the use of language – resources will be nouns (eg brand) and capabilities will be verbs (eg develop new products).
2. Human/intellectual, brand/reputational, relationships, culture and incentive systems.
3. They may overlook cross-functional capabilities such as new product development or management of strategic alliances. They can avoid this mistake by including cross-functional capabilities as a specific category or identifying capabilities based on resources.
4. Applying the VRIN/O framework is one way to do this. Valuable and rare resources will support competitive advantage, but sustained competitive advantage depends on those resources also being inimitable and non-substitutable (and exploited by the organisation). Dynamic capabilities are also a way of sustaining a competitive advantage.
5. Artefacts and behaviours, espoused values, and basic assumptions.
6. Idea time – a crucial element in being able to develop new products and processes, conflict – especially if this is political, and evaluation – too much measurement can stifle the risk-taking needed for a creative climate.
7. They both show whether an organisation is solvent – in other words, whether it can pay its creditors.
8. Because they lock them into particular ways of doing business and can make the organisation resistant to change because they represent past successes.

54

FURTHER READING

Books

Core text:

Hooley, G., Nicoulaud, B., Piercy, N. and Rudd, J. (2017) *Marketing strategy and competitive positioning*. 6th edition. Harlow, FT Prentice Hall. Chapter 6.

Supplementary texts:

Aaker, D. and McLouglin, D. (2010) *Strategic market management: global perspectives*. Chichester, John Wiley. Chapter 6.

Cravens, D.W. and Piercy, N. (2012) *Strategic marketing*. 10th edition. US, McGraw-Hill. Chapters 5 and 10.

McDonald, M. and Wilson, H. (2016) *Marketing plans: how to prepare them, how to profit from them.* 8th edition. Chichester, John Wiley. Chapter 5.

References

Aaker, D. (1991) *Managing brand equity: capitalizing on the value of a brand name*, New York, The Free Press.

Ambrosini, V., Bowman, C. and Collier, N. (2009) Dynamic capabilities: an exploration of how firms renew their resource base. *British Journal of Management*, Vol20, Supplt 1, ppS9-S24.

Anon (2014) *Hennes & Mauritz AB company profile*, London, Datamonitor.

Anthony, A. (2012) James Daunt, the bibliophile who means business. *The Guardian*, 27 May.

Barney, J. (1991) Firm resources and sustained competitive advantage. *Journal of Management.* Vol17(1), pp99–120.

Barney, J.B. and Hesterly, W.S. (2011) *Strategic management and competitive advantage*. Harlow, Pearson Higher Education.

BBC (2004) Store wars: fast fashion. *BBC News online*, 9 June. http://news.bbc.co.uk/1/hi/business/3086669.stm [accessed July 2014]

Burnside, R. (1991) Improving corporate climates for creativity. *In*: West, M.A and Farr, J.L. (Eds) *Innovation and creativity at work.* London, Wiley.

Campbell, L. (2013) Qualifications. *The Bookseller*, Iss.5564, pp4-5.

Dahlvig, A., Kling, K., and Goteman, I. (2003) IKEA CEO Anders Dahlvig on international growth and IKEA's unique corporate culture and brand identity. *The Academy of Management Executive*, Vol17(1), pp31-37.

Day, G.S. (1994) The capabilities of market-driven organisations. *Journal of Marketing*, Vol58(3), pp37-52.

Flood, A. (2013) Self-published e-book sales reach 20% of genre market. *The Guardian*, 11 June.

Foroohar, R. (2006) A new fashion frontier. *Newsweek*, 20 March.

Gap Inc. (2014) 2013 annual report, Gap Inc., San Francisco.

Ghemawat. P., and del Sol, P. (1998) Commitment versus flexibility. *California Management Review*, Vol40(4), pp26-42.

Grant, R. (2010) *Contemporary strategy analysis*. Chichester, John Wiley and Sons.

Griffiths, B. (2012) James Daunt interview. *thisismoney.co.uk*, 14 November. http://www.thisismoney.co.uk/money/markets/article-2233096/JAMES-DAUNT-INTERVIEW-Waterstones-chief-hopes-turnaround-plan-prove-real-page-turner.html [accessed July 2014]

Helfat, C., Finklestein, S., Mitchell, W., Peteraf, M., Singh, H., Teece, D., and Winter, S. (2007) *Dynamic capabilities: understanding strategic change in organisations.* US, Blackwell.

Inditex (2014) Annual report 2013, Inditex, La Coruna.

Isaksen, S. and Ekvall, G. (2010) Managing for innovation: the two faces of tension in creative climates. *Creativity and innovation management.* Vol19(2), pp73-88.

Iyer, B. and Davenport, T. (2008) Reverse engineering Google's innovation machine. *Harvard Business Review*, Vol86(4), pp58-68.

Janes, A. (2013) Case 1: reinventing Accor. *In:* Thompson, A. Strickland, L., Gamble, J., Peteraf, M., Janes, A. and Sutton, C. (2013) *Crafting and executing strategy: the quest for competitive advantage.* 1st European edition, Maidenhead, McGraw-Hill, pp456-465.

Key Note (2013) *Book retailing on the internet*, Hampton, Key Note.

Leonard-Barton, D. (1992) Core capabilities and core rigidities: a paradox in managing new product development. *Strategic Management Journal*, Vol13, Special Issue, pp111-125.

Penrose, E. (1959) *The theory of the growth of the firm*. London, Wiley.

Porter, M. (1985) *Competitive advantage*, New York, Free Press.

Rankin, J. (2013) Waterstones can live with Amazon and stem losses, says James Daunt. *The Guardian*, 4 October.

Schein, E. (2010) *Organisational culture and leadership.* San Francisco CA, Jossey-Bass.

The Economist (2009) Dynasty and durability. *The Economist*, 24 September.

Thompson, A., Strickland, L., Gamble, J., Peteraf, M., Janes, A. and Sutton, C. (2013) *Crafting and executing strategy: the quest for competitive advantage*, 1st European edition, Maidenhead, McGraw-Hill.

Wernerfelt, B. (1984) A resource-based view of the firm. *Strategic Management Journal*, Vol5(2), pp171-180.

3.

PLANNING: USING ANALYSIS AND INFORMATION TO INFORM STRATEGIC DECISION-MAKING

This chapter will help you to analyse relevant information in order to recommend and inform strategic decision-making. At the end of this chapter you will be able to:

- Undertake an audit of the external and internal marketing environments using marketing research, market intelligence and environmental scanning.
- Apply a range of relevant external analysis techniques in order to develop market insights.
- Apply a range of relevant internal analysis techniques to determine the value of an organisation's resources.
- Evaluate the implications and prioritise the importance of external and internal intelligence.

DEFINITIONS

Secondary data – "Consists of information that has been previously gathered for some purpose other than the current research project" (Wilson, 2012).

Primary data – "Data collected by a programme of observation, qualitative or quantitative research, either separately or in combination, to meet the specific objectives of a marketing research project" (Wilson, 2012).

Scenario planning – Techniques used to generate multiple narratives about the future of an organisation's external environment.

Strategic groups – Are made up of organisations within an industry that follow similar strategies or compete in the same manner.

59

3.1

GATHERING DATA FROM EXTERNAL AND INTERNAL ENVIRONMENTS

In the previous two chapters we introduced the concepts and frameworks for analysing and evaluating an organisation's external and internal environments. We will now look at how to use these to underpin the marketing planning process. We begin by looking at how to collect information to give marketers a better understanding of their organisation's internal and external environments.

Essential research methods for auditing marketing environments

There is a wide range of tools for gathering information about an organisation's internal and external environments. Each has its advantages and drawbacks, so the method you select will depend on what you want to achieve. Methods include:

- **Internal records** – For many companies, these have moved beyond traditional sales and accounts records to include customer relationship management (CRM) systems and data from websites. This information can be useful in profiling customers. Other internal records can help to identify the organisation's key resources and capabilities.
- **Desk research** – Secondary data (already published) is a prime source of information for understanding elements of the external environment – whether it's government statistics on population, information on rivals' websites or trade body data on markets and competitors. Quality can be an issue though, and marketers need to evaluate sources carefully. Secondary sources are useful for gathering information on macro-environmental factors, but are less useful for gathering data on the microenvironment.
- **Syndicated and shared research** – This can provide information cost-effectively because the data-collection process is shared. The information gathered typically generates more useful insights into customers and markets than secondary sources, over which the organisation has no control, but these insights aren't as extensive as commissioned bespoke primary research. Shared research can be useful for benchmarking exercises, which are frequently brokered by a trade association or similar industry body.
- **Bespoke primary research** – Organisations typically use this to better understand buyers, end users and competitors, and the research can be quantitative – such as surveys, experiments and observation – or qualitative – such as focus groups and in-depth interviews. It is much more expensive than the other forms of research, but it's more likely to give the organisation unique knowledge which, if it uses it effectively, can lead to competitive advantage.

Marketing research for marketing planning and strategy development

In deciding which methods to use and what data to collect and analyse marketers should keep in mind the purpose of the exercise – that is, to support the development of the organisation's strategic marketing plan. The research should be relevant and provide information that will help marketers make important decisions about marketing and corporate strategy. It also needs to underpin forecasts and objectives within the marketing plan and be capable of being used as a benchmark or baseline against which to measure the plan's progress.

Intelligence and scanning of changing market conditions

- **Competitor intelligence** – You can find information on most organisations and the products or services they offer from their websites and promotional and public relations material. Recruitment advertisements can also signal a competitor's moves. You can also gain competitor intelligence from the media (not least online) and by talking to customers and attending trade shows and other industry events. Some organisations take their surveillance of rivals even further, headhunting senior managers or key technical staff and carrying out mystery shopping on them. However, there is a fine line between acceptable and unethical behaviour in such cases.

61

> **ACTIVITY 3.1**
>
> Make a list of acceptable and unacceptable intelligence-gathering activities for your organisation. Would this list be different if you worked for another type of organisation (not-for-profit, government, commercial etc)?

- **Customer intelligence** – Many sources of competitor intelligence can yield valuable information about customers too. Trade events, for example, usually bring buyers and sellers together and are a rich source of data. They can also generate ideas for innovation, as the Real Life example overleaf illustrates.
- **The changing external environment** – Focusing on customers and competitors can provide information and knowledge that could give an organisation an advantage over less well-informed rivals. But you need to look at the wider environment too. Spotting new or potential entrants to the market or the emergence of viable substitute products requires a broader approach to intelligence gathering. Regular scanning is important too in order to anticipate major changes in the macro environment. This can be a resource-intensive process and requires support from a range of people and organisations outside the marketing department. Sales staff, agents and distributors, employees servicing key accounts and others who may have access to valuable information need a good understanding of what to look for and the kind of information they

should pass on. One way organisations can keep ahead of their rivals is by being able to read the 'weak signals' (Schoemaker and Day, 2009) in the environment, and scenario planning (covered in section 3.2) can create narratives that help those outside marketing to contribute to scanning the wider environment.

REAL LIFE 3.1

Oarsome Potential

Emily Webb is the youngest person to have appeared on *Dragons' Den* – a TV programme for would-be entrepreneurs. She was only 20 when she pitched her idea for ergonomic rowing grips to the panel in 2009. While she didn't convince any of the 'dragons' to invest, one of them, James Caan, offered her a job once she graduated. But Emily had other plans: convinced that her idea was a winner she decided to put all her time into her Oarsome Potential business.

One of the key issues Emily faced was the limited market for her product. Despite the growing popularity of rowing, fuelled in part by the UK's success in successive Olympics games, it was still a niche sport. Emily was keen to develop other markets for her product, but her limited resources put extensive market research and expensive consultancy advice out of reach.

The breakthrough came from one of her customers. He saw Emily promoting her grips at a sports trade fair and went up to talk to her – not an easy task since he had recently injured his leg and was on crutches, which he was finding difficult to use because the handles were hard. As he and Emily talked he suddenly had an idea and asked if he could borrow one of her samples. The grip fitted on the crutch and made it much easier and more comfortable to hold. That gave Emily the lead she was looking for, and following clinical trials the crutch grips are now recommended by leading physiotherapists.

This experience prompted Emily to ask her customers if they were using the grips in innovative ways on other equipment. She discovered they were using the products on hand cycles, exercise machines and off-road motorcycles, to name but three. Emily was voted Young Entrepreneur of the Year at the South Wales Business Awards in 2012, and her business continues to grow.

Demand forecasting

In order to set realistic objectives (see Chapter 4 for more detail on this) marketers need to use the data and intelligence they collect to forecast the likely demand for their organisation's products and services. This is critical in justifying the resources needed to support the plan. But to make robust forecasts they need to use a combination of sources, or their predictions may be flawed. For example, they need to take account of wider environmental factors such as inflation or net exports when forecasting industry demand, and from this they can predict sales based on market share figures.

You can carry out forecasting in a variety of ways:

- **Current demand techniques** – Such as **market build-up**, **chain ratios** and **market-factor index** methods, require a combination of internal records and external data, much of which will come from desk research.
- **Past demand methods** – Such as **time series** and **trend analysis**, are mostly based on internal records, but can be seen as naive in less stable environments. Other methods make use of models such as **innovation diffusion**, **external indicators** and **mathematical formulae**.
- **Experimental approaches** – Such as **concept testing** and **test marketing**, can provide data on which to base forecasts for new products.
- **Other approaches rely on market research** – Such as surveying buyers' intentions or the views of experts, the sales force and dealers/distributors. Such approaches are likely to be future oriented but may be subject to individual bias.

3.2

Macro-environmental analysis

We looked at some of the basic auditing techniques for assessing the organisation's macro environment in Chapter 1. But to understand the broader environment we need to move beyond basic frameworks such as PEST, especially if we're dealing with uncertain or rapidly changing environments. Marketing strategy is future oriented, so the tools and techniques we use to understand the external environment can help us to anticipate the future as well as assess the current situation.

Scenario planning is one of the most common tools. Strategy consultants, Bain and Co. (2010) estimate that over 60% of large organisations use it. Scenarios are plausible stories about the future of the organisation's environment and help the organisation to move beyond a single forecast – something that's especially important in markets experiencing significant change.

There are three principal reasons for developing future scenarios as part of the strategy process:

1. Scenarios can be used to test the robustness of different strategic options – if a particular option is suitable in most scenarios this strengthens the case for adopting it.
2. They can be used as part of an early warning system to anticipate major changes in the environment.
3. They can be used to identify future risks to a strategy and to develop contingency plans.

In order to develop scenarios an organisation needs to identify the key drivers in its external environment (a PEST or PESTELE analysis is a useful starting point), and then decide which of these are the least predictable and which have the greatest impact on the organisation. Fig 3.1 opposite shows a matrix for this activity.

ACTIVITY 3.2

Carry out a PEST analysis for an organisation that you're familiar with. Use the impact/predictability matrix to identify the key factors that you will need to research further.

You can then combine these factors using the Two Axes method (for an example, see Real Life 3.2. opposite). The extreme outcomes for the two factors (those in the high impact/low predictably quadrant) can be mapped against each other to develop a series of scenarios in the form of narratives or stories about the future. For example, the launch of a new technology might have minimal impact on sales of an organisation's product or it might make the product obsolete, and the economy might tip into recession or recover and boom – and by combining these factors we can create four possible futures against which to test our strategy or inform the future direction of the organisation. The narrative for a future where our product is obsolete and there is a recession will produce a very different strategy from the other alternatives.

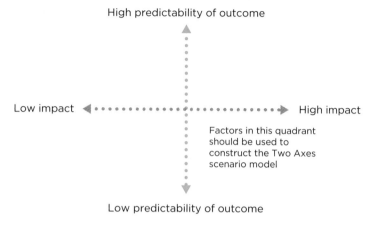

High predictability of outcome

Low impact ◄ ·······················► High impact

Factors in this quadrant should be used to construct the Two Axes scenario model

Low predictability of outcome

Fig 3.1 Impact/predictability matrix *(Source: Burt et al, 2006)*

REAL LIFE 3.2

Scenario planning in the global power industry

The Two Axes scenario matrix above was developed by managers from a large UK company that operates in the global power industry. The sector had become increasingly competitive and deregulated and senior executives wanted to understand how their increasingly volatile industry might develop in future.

The two areas they felt were least predictable, and therefore likely to have the highest impact on their business, were the nature and structure of their customers, and, because of its impact on demand for their products, the global economy. By looking at the four possible ways in which these areas could combine, the managers were able to generate four alternative future scenarios for their industry. They titled these:

* Retrenchment.
* Fill your boots.
* Survive or die.
* Win or lose.

For each of the scenarios they then produced a more detailed narrative by fleshing out a storyline. For example, the storyline for the 'win or lose' scenario talked about the growth of the global economy and of energy demand, but added that alternative energy supplies would meet much of this demand. The scenario predicted that the EU would expand its boundaries and this would produce further opportunities for the company. Against this there would be a number of mergers and acquisitions among its customers, leading to fewer more powerful buyers, which would put pressure on prices and service quality. By contrast, the 'fill your boots' scenario described a future that would allow companies to take as much as they wanted – or that growth would be substantial because of the expanding world economy.

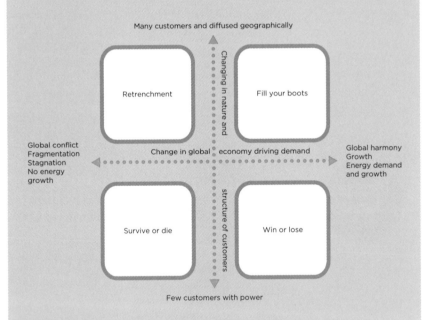

Fig 3.2 Scenario matrix for the global power industry *(Source: Burt et al, 2006)*

Micro-environmental analysis

We covered some of the key questions to ask about the firm's close environment in Chapter 1. Having established some of the basic facts and trends in the micro-environment, marketers need to use a variety of frameworks in order to turn this data and information into useful knowledge to inform the decisions they go on to make in the marketing strategy.

Starting at industry level, most marketers will be familiar with Porter's (1980) **Five Forces Framework**. But you can use a range of refinements to help you to contextualise the analysis you do using this concept.

Grundy (2006) suggests a number of refinements to make the framework of more practical value. These include:

- Combining/interrelating macro-environmental factors within the framework –which can help managers to see how some of the driving forces identified above will change the nature of their industry.
- Considering other systemic inter-dependencies – for example, can suppliers or buyers actively encourage new entrants or substitutes to enter the industry or a particular market in the industry?
- Using field force analysis to prioritise each of the five factors – which can give managers a better idea of the critical threats and the best opportunities.
- Segmenting different markets within the industry to understand variations – especially important if the organisation serves a number of the markets in an industry. For example, an automotive manufacturer might serve the luxury, family and budget car markets or the small commercial vehicle or passenger transport markets. The buyers, substitutes, potential new entrants and competitors, along with the power they wield, are likely to be very different for each of these markets.

These refinements to the framework can generate greater insight into the industry than the original, as the Real Life example below illustrates.

REAL LIFE 3.3

Extended Five Forces Framework for Spotify

We saw in Chapter 1 (Real Life 1.2) that the music industry is currently experiencing radical change, with a range of factors interacting to produce a volatile and dynamic marketplace. Spotify is an Anglo-Swedish company that provides music streaming through its website. Started in 2008 by two entrepreneurs, the company now has over 24 million users and was valued at $3 billion in 2012. It operates in a complex environment, which means it has to use a modified Five Forces Framework in order to see all the potential threats and opportunities. Fig 3.3 illustrates some of the techniques covered above in action.

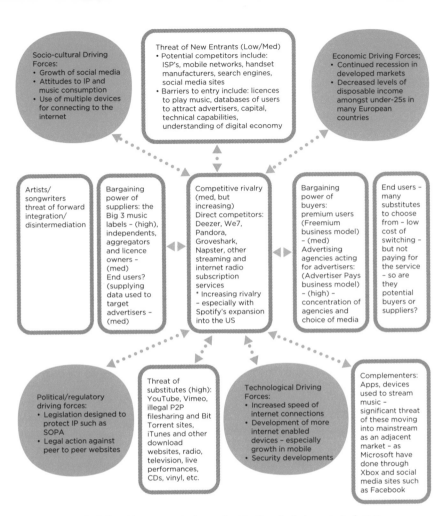

Fig 3.3 Extended Five Forces analysis applied to the digital music industry

It's important for Spotify to segment the buyers for its service because its two business models ('freemium' – that is, premium subscribers subsidise free users – and 'advertiser pays' – free users have to listen to adverts, much like a commercial radio or television channel) have very different buyers. The first segment is B2C customers who pay a monthly subscription to listen to music without adverts on an unlimited basis, and the second is B2B customers who pay for advertising to target the free users of the site.

Also, Porter's concept doesn't take account of the concept of free or illegal substitutes, something that's very important for a company like Spotify. If substitutes limit the price that firms can charge then this would appear to make the industry very unattractive – yet Spotify was able to raise substantial capital to fund its start up and unprofitable operations for several years. Economic theory would dictate that this is illogical behaviour by its backers.

Finally, the original concept of the model doesn't extend far enough along the supply and distribution chains for digital industries, where radical disintermediation is possible. If they don't examine the entire supply and distribution chain managers could miss a group of suppliers further down the chain that could leapfrog them and go direct to end consumers – in this case, artists in the music business.

A range of other tools and techniques can help you glean further insights into your industry. These include:

- **Industry/product life-cycle** – This can help with forecasting industry size and potential growth rates, but also gives an insight into the dominant strategies that could be followed at each stage of the life-cycle.
- **Strategic groups** – By analysing rivals within an industry, marketers can gain some insight into those that are closest in terms of the strategies they are following or the customer segments they are targeting. This can be a good way to identify competitive threats.
- **Trajectories of change** – It is also worth examining the extent to which the industry is changing (see Fig 3.4 below) as this can have an impact on the value of an organisation's resources and capabilities. McGahan's (2004) work on this identifies four types of industry change and the impact they have on activities (capabilities) and assets (resources).

Core assets	Core activities: Threatened	Core activities: Not threatened
Threatened	**Radical change:** Everything is up in the air	**Creative change:** The industry is constantly redeveloping assets and resources
Not threatened	**Intermediating change:** Relatonships are fragile	**Progressive change:** Companies implement incremental testing and adapt to feedback

Fig 3.4 Industry trajectories of change *(Source: McGahan, 2004)*

Insights from analysing markets and customers

McDonald and Wilson (2016) suggest four steps to audit the organisation's market;

1. Define the organisation's current markets (or markets it aspires to) and the different customer segments within these markets.
2. Determine what value customers in these markets and segments need or want.
3. Establish the extent to which competitors are meeting these needs.
4. Combine the outputs from the first three steps to determine the attractiveness of the market or segment.

Defining markets is at the heart of the process, because if you don't do this correctly the rest of the analysis – such as determining market size and growth rates – will be based on a shaky foundation. It's best to avoid product-based definitions too, and instead try to define markets and segments based on need. Techniques such as market mapping can help to generate insights into where buying decisions are made. This can be particularly important in B2B markets, where there may be a big and complex group of people in the decision-making unit for a particular product or service.

USING A RANGE OF INTERNAL ANALYSIS TECHNIQUES

We looked in some detail at organisational resources (assets) and capabilities in Chapter 2. But taking a more focused marketing perspective requires us to refine our analysis and look more closely at some aspects of the internal environment.

Analysing resources

Thompson *et al* (2013) provide a comprehensive framework for identifying resources (see Chapter 2). It's useful to explore in more depth some of the areas within the categories they list in order to pinpoint and evaluate specific marketing assets (Hooley *et al*, 2017).

- **Customer-based assets** – Such as relationships, reputation, brands, dominant market position, superior products and services.
- **Supply-chain assets** – Including control of distribution channels, unique channels, speedy delivery and security of supply, and supplier networks.
- **Internal marketing support assets** – Things like cost advantages (through the use of technology, for example), effective information systems and market intelligence, the customer base, copyrights and patents, and corporate culture.
- **Alliance-based assets** – Strategic partnerships and networks that facilitate market access, allow expertise and technology to be shared, and can be exclusive in nature.

Of all these (largely intangible assets), brands attract most attention, mainly because people view them as a guarantee of future revenue for the organisation. Brands are also traded and appear on company balance sheets, so they have a stated financial value. Specialist companies, such as Interbrand and Brand Finance, use proprietary models to value brands. The criteria such companies use can give marketers a good insight into what makes brands such valuable assets.

The Interbrand model for assessing brand strength looks at the following criteria:

Internal factors	External factors
Clarity	**Authenticity**
Clarity internally about what the brand stands for and its values, positioning, and proposition. Clarity, too, about target audiences, customer insights and drivers. Because so much hinges on this, it is vital that these things are articulated and shared across the organisation.	The brand is soundly based on an internal truth and capability. It has a defined heritage and a well-grounded value set. It can deliver against the (high) expectations that customers have of it.

Commitment	Relevance
Internal commitment to brand, and a belief internally in the importance of brand. The extent to which the brand receives support in terms of time, influence and investment.	The fit with customer/consumer needs, desires and decision criteria across all relevant demographics and geographies.
Protection	Differentiation
How secure the brand is across a number of dimensions, including legal protection, proprietary ingredients or design, scale and geographic spread.	The degree to which customers/consumers perceive the brand to have a distinct and differentiated positioning from the competition.
Responsiveness	Consistency
The ability to respond to market changes, challenges and opportunities. The brand should have a sense of leadership internally, and a desire and ability to constantly evolve and renew itself.	The degree to which a brand is experienced without fail across all touchpoints or formats.
	Presence
	The degree to which a brand feels omnipresent and is talked about positively by consumers, customers and opinion formers in both traditional and social media.
	Understanding
	Customers not only recognise the brand, but also have an in-depth knowledge and understanding of its distinctive qualities and characteristics. (Where relevant, this will extend to consumers' understanding of the company that owns the brand.)

Fig 3.5 The Interbrand model for assessing brand strength (*Source:* Adapted from an excerpt of Interbrand's Best Global Brands Methodology as found at www.interbrand.com/en/best-global-brands/2013/best-blobal-brands-methodology.aspx)

Brand valuation companies combine such factors with financial analysis and other criteria to create annual lists of leading global brands. Valuation methodologies have changed in recent years to take account of shifts in the environment, and this has led to technology brands such as Google and Microsoft overtaking some of the older more established brands, such as car manufacturers and FMCG products such as Coca-Cola, on the valuation companies' lists.

Analysing capabilities

As we saw in Chapter 2, you can find capabilities at all levels in the organisation. Some are single tasks that the organisation excels at and others require the co-operation of several different parts of the business. **Marketing capabilities** can be divided into four categories (Hooley *et al*, 2017):

- Product and service management.
- Pricing and tendering.
- Advertising, promotion and selling.
- Distribution and logistics.

These provide the core functional capabilities for the organisation in the marketing area and can be assessed in the same way as other skills and abilities through applying the VRIN criteria we looked at in Chapter 2.

Wang and Ahmed (2007) have added a set of 'dynamic capabilities' covering:

- Absorptive capability – the capacity for effective market sensing and learning to modify routines and processes in response to changes in the environment.
- Adaptive capability – the ability to see and exploit market opportunities.
- Innovative capability – the ability to develop new products and services.

Resources and capabilities are linked and each organisation owns or controls a portfolio of assets and abilities. While the VRIN framework is useful in evaluating individual resources and capabilities, to appreciate the bigger picture we also need to look at the organisation's portfolio as a whole.

Grant (2010) suggests assessing each resource and capability using two criteria – relative strength compared with competitors, and strategic importance (that is, the extent to which it can confer a sustained advantage over rivals). You could modify this for a marketing context (Hooley *et al*, 2017) by looking at the strategic importance of the resource or capability in creating customer value.

You can then score each resource and capability against the two criteria (a scale of 1 to 10 – with 1 being very low and 10 very high – is one way to do this). The data and information from the research conducted and intelligence gathered to underpin the strategic marketing plan can inform this process. For example, benchmarking can help to assess the relative strength of an asset, and the VRIN criteria can help to determine the level of competitive advantage a resource or capability enjoys. However, this is not an easy task and you will always have to make some assumptions and use judgement and interpretation – with all the risks this involves (see Chapter 1).

Finally, you can plot the portfolio on a matrix (see Fig 3.5 below) and this can inform the way you manage each resource and capability, whether in terms of exploiting key strengths or deciding what to do about significant weaknesses.

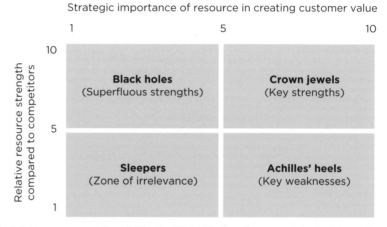

Strategic importance of resource in creating customer value

| | 1 | 5 | 10 |

Black holes
(Superfluous strengths)

Crown jewels
(Key strengths)

Sleepers
(Zone of irrelevance)

Achilles' heels
(Key weaknesses)

Relative resource strength compared to competitors

10

5

1

Fig 3.5 Resource and Capability Portfolio Matrix *(Sources: Adapted from Grant, 2010 and Hooley et al., 2017).*

CASE STUDY 3.1

Nike's portfolio of resources and capabilities

In 2012 Nike reached the top of the US Patent Board's Consumer Products scorecard, confirming its status as one of the most innovative companies in the world. New products have been at the heart of the firm's success since it was founded in 1964 by sports coach Bill Bowerman and college runner Phil Knight with the aim of producing better shoes for runners.

Much of Nike's early growth was organic and limited to North American markets, but in the late 1980s it embarked on a series of acquisitions designed to build a portfolio of brands and products similar to some of its European rivals. It bought Cole Haan in 1988 and Bauer Hockey in 1994, and in 2002 it diversified into surf-wear with the acquisition of Hurley International. Nike's strategy of buying other firms in order to grow its market share in footwear and apparel accelerated after 2000 with the purchase of Converse in 2003, Starter in 2004 and Umbro in 2008. But it managed its portfolio aggressively and where the prospects for market growth looked unattractive it divested brands – Starter in 2007, Bauer Hockey in 2008 (the US ice hockey market looked flat), Umbro in 2012 and Cole Haan in 2013.

The company's most recent developments are still linked to items people wear but have crossed over into technology applications and services. For example, the Fuel Band, launched in 2012, is a wearable technology that records an individual's movements during the day and allows them to download the data to a computer or smartphone to help them with their training and fitness regime.

By 2012 the firm employed significant numbers of specialists in a wide range of fields, from biomechanics to chemistry, exercise physiology to product design. Nike involved users of its products through a series of research committees and advisory boards, populated by trainers, athletes and coaches, which allowed it to maintain its connection with sports groups. Medical stakeholders, including podiatrists and orthopaedists, were also involved in the committees.

In addition to its skill in portfolio management and innovation, Nike had also demonstrated considerable ability in strategic marketing. Its use of sponsorship and branding, for example, has always set it apart from its competitors in terms of image. The Nike brand and distinctive swoosh logo first appeared in the early 1970s and its sponsorship of another US athlete, Steve Prefontaine, gave the brand national prominence. The firm went on to develop links with other leading sports stars, such as Michael Jordan, and its close links to sport and athletes made it well placed to identify future stars: it backed Tiger Woods when he was up and coming, for example. Retail outlets were important to the firm almost from the outset, and Nike has sustained its retail presence through the development of direct-to-consumer online retailing. In 2012 the firm controlled 826 retail outlets, but sold wholesale to many thousands more, in over 190 countries, making it the largest seller of athletic apparel in the world.

ACTIVITY 3.3

Using the Nike case study, identify the company's resources and capabilities and estimate how strong they are compared with competitors such as Adidas and Puma and how important they might be in creating value for the firm's customers. Use the Portfolio Matrix above to plot each resource and capability you have scored. What does this tell you about the company?

PRIORITISE AND JUSTIFY KEY ISSUES

We have covered the research methods, sources of data and some of the key tools for analysing the external and internal environments. Applying these frameworks can help us to turn the data collected into information and draw logical conclusions from it. But to turn this information into usable knowledge, we need to carry out further activities.

The Marketing Information System

A Marketing or Management Information System (MKIS or MIS) is a tool for bringing together a range of information from disparate sources to create knowledge and insights into the organisation's environment that can benefit a variety of different users (see Fig 3.6 below for a generic example). These systems should provide knowledge that will help people at all levels in the organisation to make more effective decisions. But the inputs and outputs need to be tailored to ensure that the right data and information is collected and the right knowledge and insights are disseminated to relevant users.

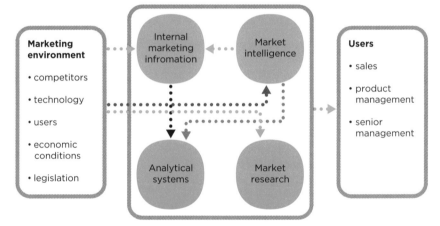

Figure 3.6 Generic Marketing Information System

SWOT and TOWS analysis

In order to communicate the analysis underpinning a strategic plan succinctly, managers need to synthesise the findings. One of the most common tools used in strategic planning is the Strengths, Weaknesses, Opportunities and Threats (SWOT) framework, which summaries the key issues arising from the audit and analysis of the organisation's external environment. By focusing on the organisation's most important strengths and weaknesses and the key opportunities and threats, marketers can start to see how best to deploy their resources and capabilities. However, the framework is deceptively simple and most SWOT analyses are too general and too long (Hill and Westbrook, 1997).

Coman and Ronen (2009) suggest that an effective SWOT should be:

- **Concise** – With no more than four or five factors listed against each of the categories.
- **Authentic** – The factors listed should be supported by strong evidence from the audit and analysis and treated objectively, rather than ending up as a 'wish-list' that bears little relation to reality.
- **Significant** – The factors should have a substantial impact on the value of the organisation.
- **Actionable** – The factors should provide a clear call to action so objectives can be set to remedy the weaknesses, exploit the opportunities and so on.

McDonald and Wilson (2016) provide useful guidance on how to perform this difficult exercise successfully by clearly defining the parameters for each category.

Strengths	Weaknesses
• It can create value for the organisation/customer • It is unique • It is inimitable • It is lasting	• It is meaningful to the customer • It is unique • It is difficult to fix
Opportunities	**Threats**
• It is large • It is accessible • It is lasting	• It is significant • It is lasting

Figure 3.7 Guidelines for a meaningful SWOT *(Source: McDonald and Wilson, 2016 p.145)*

ACTIVITY 3.4

Source a SWOT analysis from your organisation or one that you know well. Apply Coman and Ronen's, and McDonald and Wilson's criteria to the factors within the SWOT. How well do they meet these parameters? (If you can't find a SWOT within your organisation there are many examples online. Just enter 'example SWOT analysis' or something similar.

One of the other criticisms of the SWOT framework is that it doesn't show the relationships between the different factors and categories – for example, when a particular threat could make a weakness more significant. In order to remedy this and to help with generating strategic actions, Heinz Weihrich developed the TOWS model to enhance the SWOT. TOWS matches each internal category to the external factors to create four strategy choice sets:

Strengths/Threats or 'maxi-mini' strategy options – Managers need to think about which organisational strengths can mitigate or lessen threats in the external environment.

Strengths/Opportunities or 'maxi-maxi' strategy options – Managers should look at which organisational strengths can be used to exploit opportunities in the external environment.

Weaknesses/Opportunities or 'mini-maxi' strategy options – Managers should concentrate on which organisational weaknesses need to be addressed in order to be able to exploit opportunities in the external environment.

Weaknesses/Threats or 'mini-mini' strategy options – Managers need to focus on which organisational weaknesses need to be addressed and which external threats mitigated.

QUICK QUIZ – CHECK YOUR KNOWLEDGE

Questions
1. What research methods could you use to audit the marketing environment?
2. What are the main uses of scenario planning?
3. For what type of industries might you need to use a Modified Five Forces Framework?
4. What are the four characteristics that Coman and Ronen believe are indicative of a good SWOT?

Answers
1. Company records, desk research, syndicated/shared research, bespoke primary research.
2. To test strategies, to identify risks, to anticipate major changes in the external environment.
3. Those with multiple markets served by the same competitors, those where radical disintermediation is possible due to internet business models.
4. Concise, Authentic, Significant, Actionable.

FURTHER READING

Books

Core text:

Hooley, G., Nicoulaud, B., Piercy, N. and Rudd, J. (2017) *Marketing strategy and competitive positioning*. 6th edition. Harlow, FT Prentice Hall. Chapters 1-7.

Supplementary texts:

Aaker, D. and McLouglin, D. (2010) *Strategic market management: global perspectives*. Chichester, John Wiley. Chapters 1-6.

Cravens, D.W. and Piercy, N. (2012) *Strategic marketing*. 10th edition. US, McGraw-Hill. Chapters 1, 2, 4 and 5.

McDonald, M. and Wilson, H. (2016) *Marketing plans: how to prepare them, how to profit from them*. 8th edition. Chichester, John Wiley. Chapters 1-5.

References

Bain (2010) *Management tools and trends*. Bain and Company, Boston, MA.

Burt, G., Wright, G., Bradfield, R., Cairns, G. and Van Der Heijden, K. (2006) The role of scenario planning in exploring the environment in view of the limitations of PEST and its derivatives. *International Studies of Management and Organisation*, Vol36(3), pp50-76.

Coman, A. and Ronen, B. (2009) Focused SWOT: diagnosing critical strengths and weaknesses. *International Journal of Production Research*, Vol47(20), pp5677-5689.

Grundy, T. (2006) Rethinking and reinventing Michael Porter's Five Forces model. *Strategic Change*, Vol15(5), pp213-29.

Hill, T. and Westbrook, R. (1997) SWOT analysis: It's time for a product recall. *Long Range Planning*, Vol30(1), pp46-52.

Interbrand (2014) *Best global brands 2013*. Interbrand. www. bestglobalbrands.com [accessed July 2014]

McGahan, A. (2004) How industries change. *Harvard Business Review*, October, pp86-94.

Weihrich, H. (1982) The TOWS Matrix – a tool for situational analysis. *Long Range Planning*, Vol15(2), pp54-66.

Wilson, A. (2012) *Marketing research: an integrated approach*. Harlow, FT Prentice Hall.

4.
PLANNING: DEVELOPING STRATEGIC MARKETING PLANS

OUTLINE

This chapter will help you to develop a strategic marketing plan to realise organisational objectives. By the end of the chapter you will be able to:

- Create a range of justifiable goals that reflect the external and internal contexts of an organisation.
- Identify and evaluate alternative strategic options for delivering market value.
- Recommend and justify strategic decisions based on market intelligence and the internal dynamics of an organisation.
- Present tactical recommendations that are justifiable and are aligned with strategic decisions.

DEFINITIONS

Vision – "A strategic vision describes management's aspirations for the future and delineates the organisation's strategic course and long-term direction." (Thompson *et al*, 2013)

Mission – Defines the boundaries of the organisation's operations and its overall purpose.

Objectives – The intended and precise outcomes of a strategy.

Generic strategies – "Prescriptions about what the content of a firm's strategy should be." (Bowman, 2008)

Best cost/cost innovation – Hybrid strategies that successfully combine cost-leadership or low-price approaches with a differentiated position.

Balanced scorecard – A system that provides managers with a combination of quantitative and qualitative measures, relevant to all stakeholders of the organisation.

STRATEGIC MARKETING GOALS AND OBJECTIVES

As we have seen, the strategic planning process in its most basic form is about answering three questions – where are we now? where do we want to go? how are we going to get there? The audit and analysis element of the process addresses the where we are now issue, so the next element to consider is where we want to go. There are a number of levels to this, and the functional (in this case marketing) strategy is one of them (see Fig 4.1 for details). Also, within the marketing strategy there are overarching strategic decisions and tactical choices, all of which need to display some degree of fit with the organisation's overall strategy or, at the very least, be consistency with its long-term direction.

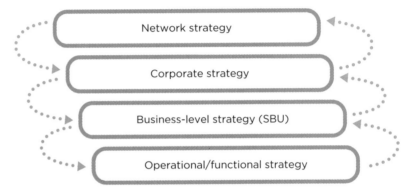

Fig 4.1 Levels of strategy *(Sources: Thompson et al, 2013; De Wit and Meyer, 2010)*

Mission/vision statements – The first step for most strategic planning processes is the mission or vision statement. According to Thompson *et al* (2013) we should distinguish between the vision – which is an aspiration for the future direction of the organisation – and the mission – which should describe its purpose. The main problem with both mission and vision statements is that they tend to be bland and generic rather than distinctive and meaningful.

REAL LIFE 4.1

World Horse Welfare's vision, mission and values

UK-based charity World Horse Welfare went through a major re-branding exercise in 2008 and recast its vision, mission and values as follows.

Our vision: World Horse Welfare's vision is a world where every horse is treated with respect, compassion and understanding.

Our mission: Our mission is to work with horses, horse owners, communities, organisations and governments to help improve welfare standards and stamp out suffering in the UK and worldwide.

Our values: In everything we do, we aim to be:

- Realistic in our approach, focusing on the practical to achieve what is possible now while mindful of the future.
- Compassionate in our attitudes, behaviour and decision-making.
- Forward-thinking in anticipating challenge and change, always seeking new ways of being more effective.

Like many not-for-profit organisations its vision is very clear, forward looking and aspirational – though whether it is truly achievable is debatable. The mission statement clearly sets out the purpose of the organisation and the boundaries it operates within. The charity's vision, mission and values appear to be distinctive. However, when you compare them with those of other charities in the same sector, such as Brooke Hospital, Redwings and Blue Cross, you can see clear similarities.

(Source: World Horse Welfare, 2014)

Corporate objectives – These are objectives that cover the organisation's overall direction and are often expressed in financial terms – such as an increase in profits or shareholder value. As we saw in Chapter 2, return on capital employed is a key ratio, but earnings per share (EPS) is another popular measure. There should be a clear link between these high-level objectives and the functional and business unit objectives. Some organisations are increasingly using frameworks such as the balanced scorecard in order to focus on a range of outcomes rather than just financial performance.

Strategic marketing objectives – These objectives will cover outcomes regarding products and markets – typical objectives could include increasing market share, developing a better known brand than rivals or being first to market with product or service innovations, for example. These might sit at business level or functional level (see Fig 4.1 opposite) depending on the organisational context.

SMART objectives – In all but the smallest organisations objectives will need to be communicated to a wide range of staff and other stakeholders. Whether they are overarching corporate goals or specific objectives for a marketing strategy they need to be clearly stated and unambiguous, or they could be misinterpreted.

One way of achieving this is to use the SMART criteria:

- **Specific** – Avoid general or vague objectives such as 'increase sales'. Be precise about the outcomes required.
- **Measurable** – Where possible objectives should be capable of being quantified so that you can assess performance against them.
- **Assignable** – A designated person or team should be responsible for the objective. (In some versions of SMART this element is labelled 'Achievable', but this then misses out the responsibility aspect, which in itself is important to how achievable an objective is.)
- **Realistic** – The objectives should not be wishful thinking. They need to be attainable with the resources allocated or they can become very demotivating.
- **Time bound** – You should specify a date by which the objective needs to be achieved.

An example of a SMART marketing objective might be:

'The international marketing team will increase our share of the global market for widgets from 23% to 26% over the next 12 months.'

ACTIVITY 4.1

Look for objectives in a range of documents for the organisation you work for or one you have researched. Annual reports, shareholder briefings, business or marketing strategies and plans may all be useful starting points. Are the objectives in these documents SMART? If they are, look at how the different criteria are manifested. If the objectives aren't SMART, use the criteria to try to make them SMART.

4.2

STRATEGIC CHOICES

The decisions managers make about the future direction of the organisation lie at the heart of any strategy. Most managers focus on two aspects – **where** the organisation should operate or compete and **how** it will compete (or be distinctive from its rivals). More recently, organisations have also started to consider who they will work with, as networks, alliances and other forms of strategic partnership have become more important.

Where to compete

Traditionally people have tended to think in terms of markets and products when making decisions about the scope of the organisation's operations. The growth matrix developed by Igor Ansoff (1988) presents managers with a set of choices and details the risks associated with each. The least risky growth path is to stick with existing products in current markets – a strategy of **market penetration**. By contrast, growing through launching new products into new markets – or **diversification** – is the highest-risk option, although it can also produce the most significant returns, especially if the organisation is a first mover in the field or can create a 'blue ocean'. Managers need to weigh up the risks and returns for each option – and we will look at how to evaluate the different options in more detail below.

REAL LIFE 4.2

Adidas' decisions on where to compete

Adidas was founded in the late 1940s by Adi Dassler. The firm started by producing athletic footwear for the German market, but the brand became international as a result of its links to the Olympic movement (at the 1972 Munich Games over 80% of the athletes wore Adidas shoes) and built strong sales in Europe and the US. Adidas diversified into clothing in the 1970s, which enabled it to move into new markets by appealing to teenagers as well as serious athletes. In the 1990s it moved into sports equipment too through the acquisition of companies such as Salomon, TaylorMade Golf and Mavic, a bicycle components company. However, most of these new businesses did not perform well and Adidas sold several of them in 2005. During the 1990s Adidas also expanded its company-owned stores. In 2006 it acquired rival athletic footwear and apparel brand Reebok, which allowed it to grow in markets such as South America.

Adidas has changed the scope of its business through market penetration, product development and market development. The move into specialist sports equipment could be seen as a 'related diversification' – but this proved the least successful of its moves and demonstrates that the further a firm gets from its existing markets and products, the higher the risk of failure. The move into retail is an example of 'forward vertical integration' and exposes the limitations of Ansoff's matrix in that it doesn't cover choices about the scope of the organisation.

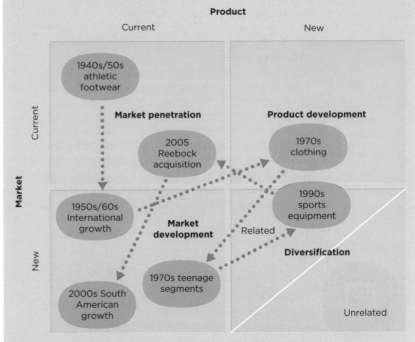

Fig 4.2 Ansoff's (1988) product/market growth matrix applied to Adidas' strategic decisions

How to compete

As we saw in Chapter 2, resources and capabilities that are difficult to imitate, or are unique in some way, support and sustain an organisation's competitive advantage over its rivals. In order to focus on the right activities and assets, marketers have to make choices about how they will compete. Michael Porter (1980) proposed a set of generic ways in which organisations compete.

1. By being the **lowest-cost supplier** in a market an organisation can generate higher margins than its rivals by charging the same price and reinvesting the surplus, or it can attract a higher volume of customers by charging a lower price.
2. An organisation can **differentiate itself** from rivals in a range of ways, from offering unique product or service features, to using exclusive distribution channels or developing strong customer

loyalty through branding. This allows the organisation to charge higher prices to customers or charge the same price as rivals and benefit from a higher volume of sales due to the higher perceived value of its product or service.

3. Finally, an organisation can focus on a single niche or small number of segments in a market and position itself as the lowest-cost provider or take a differentiated position as described above.

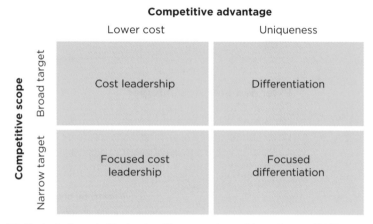

Competitive advantage

		Lower cost	Uniqueness
Competitive scope	Broad target	Cost leadership	Differentiation
	Narrow target	Focused cost leadership	Focused differentiation

Fig 4.3 Porter's Generic Strategies *(Source: adapted from Porter, 1980)*

Porter (1980) stated that managers needed to make a clear decision about the scope of business activities and the form of competitive advantage to select. At all costs, he believed, an organisation should avoid being 'stuck in the middle'. However, the combination of increasing globalisation, deregulation and disruptive changes to a wide variety of markets through technical innovation has led people to question and criticise this view, along with many of the other assumptions underpinning Porter's work.

CASE STUDY 4.1

Swatch's differentiation strategy and integrated marketing mix

Swiss watch manufacturer Swatch is recognised as a global leader in the sector. To support its strategy of differentiation the company has integrated its marketing mix as follows:

- **Place** – It is selective about channels to market, focusing on jewellers, department stores and airport shops so as to maintain a certain degree of exclusivity.
- **Promotion** – It maintains a high spend on marketing in order to support the brand.

- **Price** – Although some lines cost as little as £40 the watches are relatively highly priced compared with other players in the same strategic group.
- **Product** – The firm puts a great deal of resource into innovation and product design. The modern and unusual designs, which it changes frequently, have sustained the brand's cult status and created a 'collectors' market'.

Recent figures confirm the success of this strategic approach. Swatch's half-year gross sales for Quarters 1 and 2 2014 were up 8.5%, with an operating margin of 20.2%.

Extended generic strategies

Several alternative approaches to generic strategy development (Bowman, 1996; Williamson, 2010) provide examples of firms that have successfully combined low price or low cost with a differentiated customer value proposition. Increasingly, companies from emerging economies such as India, China, Brazil and Russia are able to use

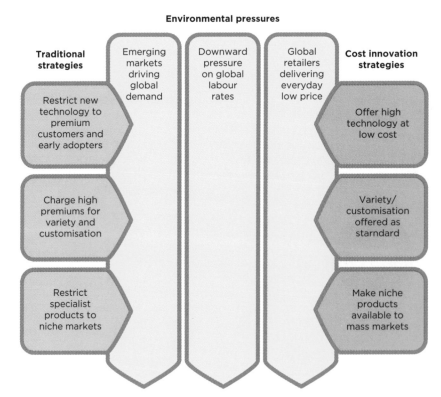

Fig 4.4 Cost innovation *(Source: Williamson, 2010)*

their low cost base to produce customised or high-specification products and offer them at a lower price than rivals in Europe and North America. Chinese domestic appliance firm Haier, for example, successfully entered the US market by supplying value-for-money products through Walmart. This strategy is referred to as 'best cost' (Thompson *et al*, 2013) or 'cost innovation' (Williamson, 2010). Technological advances mean that firms in developed economies are increasingly able to adopt this approach– as the Real Life example opposite demonstrates.

REAL LIFE 4.3

Les Nouveaux Ateliers – cost innovation in action

When they were students Francois Chambaud and Nicolas Wolfovski used to talk about the limits of off-the-peg clothes. It annoyed them that everyone wore the same clothes and it was difficult to stand out from the crowd unless you were wealthy and could afford made-to-measure. What would the world be like, they wondered, if they could find a way to give everyone access to this élite world of bespoke tailoring?

They knew that it was possible to have a tailor-made suit or shirt made in Hong Kong or Singapore for a much lower price than in Paris or London – but the cost of air travel and accommodation made this as expensive as the local French tailoring.

In February 2010, Paris Charles de Gaulle airport introduced full-body scanners, to collect and digitise the details of passengers to the United States for security purposes. What if, wondered Chambaud and Wolfovski, that technology could be adapted to measure someone's body instead of looking for hidden weapons?

A year later, in 2011, the pair set up a men's clothing store, based in Paris, called Les Nouveaux Ateliers ('The New Workshop'). It was the first business to use 3D imaging techniques in tailoring, and used scanners to take up to 200 body measurements and generate a digital template of the customer in a fraction of the time it took a traditional bespoke tailor to do the same thing. Clients could then choose the pattern, fabric, cut, buttons and all the other details of their clothes, and the specifications were sent electronically to Shanghai for manufacture. Finally the finished clothes were shipped back to France.

The whole process took three weeks as opposed to the three months it normally takes to make a made-to-measure suit. Even better, the company could sell the bespoke suits at mass-market prices. This is an example of the 'cost innovation' revolution that is happening in production, consigning the old rule – that customised products can only be made at high cost – to the dustbin. A wide range of companies are now using technology and global supply chains to give customers what they really want rather than what the firm thinks it can deliver.

Many ways to differentiate
Managers also need to think about how they will compete at a detailed level. On what basis will they differentiate their product or service offering? Porter (1980) talked in terms of 'uniqueness drivers' (and described the different factors that might support a cost leadership position as 'cost drivers'). Other strategists have argued that all positions in the marketplace are differentiated (Mintzberg, 1998) because customers don't see cost leadership; all they see is either a low price or something they perceive of higher value than a similarly-priced offering by a competitor.

Mintzberg classified sources of differentiation into six categories:

- Price
- Image
- Support
- Quality
- Design
- Undifferentiated

The final category acknowledges what most executives have always known – that you can adopt a copycat strategy and still make fair returns. The most successful strategies tend to combine several different sources of differentiation and/or cost advantage.

Strategic options in difficult market conditions
We have already seen how global markets, deregulation and large-scale retailers have enabled firms in emerging economies to challenge established players in developed economies. These new entrants have created difficult market conditions for the incumbents. Tackling low-priced or low-cost competitors can mean an organisation has to take tough decisions – including cutting its own prices or investing heavily to deepen its differentiation. Other options include launching low-cost subsidiaries – as Fitness First, the international gym and health club group, did in the UK with its Klick Fitness brand.

Other difficult market conditions can include 'hypercompetitive' (D'Aveni, 1994) or 'high velocity' sectors where the pace of disruptive innovation (often due to new technologies) can rapidly undermine a firm's market position. Organisations in these situations have to take a short-term view of product life-cycles and be willing to cannibalise even very successful products (software is one example of this). But smaller moves, misleading the competition and behaving unpredictably are options too.

Segmentation, targeting, positioning
Once you've decided where and how to compete in broad terms you need to focus on the markets and sub-markets you are going to serve.

You can **segment** markets in a variety of ways, but in essence segmentation is about splitting a market into different groups of customers with similar needs, selecting particular targets to focus on and positioning the organisation's offer to appeal to these customers by best meeting their needs. Segmenting markets can often produce increased profits, but it also helps to retain customers because marketers' understanding of different parts of the market means they can tailor the value proposition more precisely for different groups.

Once you've identified viable segments – that is, discrete groups that respond to a particular marketing mix in a unique and consistent manner and have the potential to provide the organisation with acceptable returns – you need to decide which ones to **target**. Your decision will be based on a variety of factors but the ones you choose to target will also be those to which the organisation's resources and capabilities are best suited. Once again, the internal and external analysis you've already done (and covered in previous chapters) will help to inform this process.

You then need to look at how to **position** the organisation to compete in your designated target markets. Techniques such as 'perceptual mapping' can help. Again there are a number of alternatives to choose from, and Chapters 2 and 7 in the core text (Hooley, Piercy, Nicoulaud and Rudd, 2017) cover these in depth and provide a good overview of the principles involved.

Other strategic considerations
The core text and supplementary books cover a number of additional aspects of strategic marketing, and each of these will generate a set of choices and require decisions to be made. We list some examples below:

- **Brand strategies** – Whether organisations choose to operate corporate brands, such as Heinz, range brands, such as Ford, multi-branding, such as Procter and Gamble and Unilever (although both of these firms are increasingly adopting a mixed approach), or even if they choose not to brand at all and offer generic products, brand strategy decisions have implications for the rest of the marketing plan and need to be articulated explicitly. Other strategies for brands include extension and stretching. Virgin, for example, has stretched its brand from records to airlines, bridal shops and cosmetics, and UK supermarkets are increasingly following suit with moves into banking and mobile telecoms.

- **Profit and sales projections** – We will cover these further when we look at operational metrics in Chapter 6, but, to summarise, marketers need to have made decisions about how much revenue and profit the marketing plan will produce in order to be able to assess how well the strategy is performing. In reality what appears in the plan is normally the guaranteed projection, and will therefore be quite conservative. Projections based on stretch targets will usually be used as the basis for contingency plans to be put into place if the market grows dramatically. In mature markets it may be relatively easy to make these projections, but in industries that are declining, growing or emerging you need to pay more attention to analysing the environment to ensure your predictions are underpinned by robust logic.

- **Social and ethical implications** – Organisations are increasingly being held accountable for their activities by a range of stakeholders, as we discussed in Chapter 1 and will examine further in Chapter 5. As such, 'triple bottom line' targets (Elkington, 1999) are becoming an important element of both corporate and marketing strategic objectives. Marketers also need to think about whether there is advantage to be gained from matching their organisation's value proposition with the social and ethical values of the segments they target. Innocent Drinks, Ben and Jerry's and Body Shop have all found this a strong position.

- **Relationship and one-to-one marketing** – These concepts have been important in consumer marketing since the 1990s – and even earlier in B2B markets. But the internet has given this element of marketing further impetus as the relationship between organisations, their brands and consumers has gone online, where it presents significant threats as well as opportunities. As we saw in Chapter 1 by reference to the Seven Markets model, a variety of stakeholder markets can have an impact on customers and their relationship with the organisation. However, relationship marketing techniques are not appropriate for all products and purchases – so here again marketers need to make choices based on their analysis of the context.

4.3 RECOMMENDING AND JUSTIFYING STRATEGIC DECISIONS

Once you've generated a set of options you have to choose which path to follow in order to allocate resources efficiently and to configure the organisation to support the position adopted. For example, companies following a cost-leadership strategy will often incentivise staff to save money wherever possible. In order to justify any changes proposed and additional resources requested to support the plan, managers need to provide robust justification for their recommendations. This can involve using a range of tools to help rank the possible options and choose between them. These might include:

- Evaluation matrices
- Suitability, feasibility and acceptability
- Cultural fit
- Associated risk
- Return on marketing investment
- Stakeholder expectations
- Strategic logic

In essence, managers need to be able to evaluate the level of fit the strategy has with the internal and external environments, the level of projected performance (usually in terms of risk and return) that will meet key stakeholder expectations, and the competitive advantage the strategy is likely to produce.

Johnson, Whittington and Scholes's (2011) Suitability, Acceptability, Feasibility method provides an overarching framework that you could use to score strategic options.

- **Suitability** – Can be assessed by determining how well the strategy fits with the internal and external environments. Evaluation matrices – such as the Shell Directional Policy matrix, TOWS analysis or scenario planning (covered in Chapter 3 above) can underpin this and provide robust data to help justify the recommended choice.
- **Acceptability** – Includes a range of performance measures. These might be financial (the risks and returns for a particular strategy, for example) but may also cover a range of marketing, innovation, learning and operational measures if these are collected using a scorecard or dashboard system (see Chapter 6 for more on measuring strategic performance). Different stakeholders will have different views on what is acceptable in terms of strategy performance, so you could also use this element of evaluation to consider whether the expectations of the different groups who have influence over the strategy are being met (or need to be met).
- **Feasibility** – Covers practical matters related to resources and capabilities. Does the organisation have the finances, people and skills to deliver the strategy that is being proposed?

Strategic logic

A number of competing frameworks are available to add additional dimensions to the evaluation of strategic options. Rumelt (1980), for example, adds Consistency as a key determinant – in other words, is the strategy consistent with the organisation's goals and purpose? Strategic logic is about this fit with the mission and values of the organisation – but it also needs to take account of the key abilities and skills of the organisation and its staff. Nicholson (1995) suggests combining the two elements using a matrix approach (see Fig 4.5 below). Managers need to answer two questions in order to evaluate each option, he says:

1. How well does it fit with, and help achieve, the firm's mission?
2. How well does it use and further develop the firm's core competencies? *(Nicholson, 1995, p5)*

The options, once plotted on the Mission and Core Competence (MCC) matrix, can then inform the decision-making process. Options in the Drive quadrant will be given priority for resources and execution, while choices plotted in the dilution or distraction quadrants might be pursued through strategic alliances or subsidiary companies.

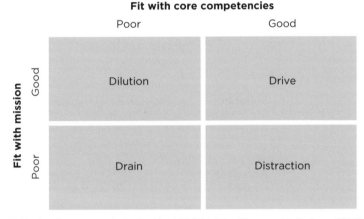

Fig 4.5 Evaluating strategic logic: the MCC Matrix *(Source: Nicholson, 1995)*

4.4

TACTICS

Within a strategic marketing plan, the tactical elements will tend to be detailed for the first year and then for the remaining period of the strategy provided only in outline. Tactics are the operational marketing mix activities that companies use to achieve their strategic objectives (see Case Study 4.1 above, on Swatch, for an illustration of this). The traditional 4Ps marketing mix (Product, Promotion, Price and Place), first conceptualised in the 1960s, has been supplemented by the additional 3Ps of People, Process and Physical Evidence as a result of the growth of the service sector in developed economies. Service, not goods, is now the dominant paradigm in marketing (Vargo and Lusch, 2004). The internet has further complicated many of the mix elements as virtual and real worlds become increasingly integrated, and future developments such as 3D printing and the Internet of Things will provide even more challenges and opportunities.

This section will look briefly at the various elements of the extended marketing mix (the 7Ps) but you should read it in conjunction with one of the recommended textbooks in order to fully understand its place in the strategic planning process.

Pricing plans – As with all elements of the marketing mix these should support the chosen position and integrate with the other tactical plans outlined below. Pricing is a difficult part of the mix and can often bring marketing into conflict with other parts of the organisation – especially the accounting or finance functions.

Pricing tactics need to take into account a range of factors:

- Production costs
- Value to the customer over the lifetime of the product ('economic value')
- Prices charged by competitors
- Positioning
- Overall business objectives
- Elasticity of demand

There are several methods for actually setting the price, including:

- Perceived-value pricing
- Going-rate pricing
- Cost-plus pricing

However, there will also be occasions when you need to use promotional pricing tactics, such as pricing a product as a loss leader to encourage purchase of other more valuable products or services. Part of the reason for the disputes between Amazon and major publishers such as Hachette is that the latter believe Amazon is offering books at loss-leading prices in order to attract customers to its website where they buy more valuable products such as consumer electronics. The key issue to consider with pricing is whether it supports the overarching position for the product or service. In the Swatch example above, for example, we saw how maintaining a relatively high price supports its differentiation strategy.

Promotional plans – These include decisions about the message and communication tools as well as which media to use and what budget to allocate to this part of the mix. Marketers will need to specify within the promotional plan what proportion of the promotional budget will be allocated to different aspects of the promotional mix – advertising, public relations, sales promotions, personal selling, direct marketing and sponsorship.

Distribution plans – These should cover how the product or service is delivered to the customer. Is it delivered direct or via an intermediary, such as a wholesaler or retailer, for example? The internet has had a profound effect on this aspect of the marketing mix.

Product plans – These will include both the management of the existing product portfolio and varying degrees of new product development, from repackaging existing lines to new-to-the-world innovations. Existing product decisions can be driven by portfolio analysis using tools such as the GE Multi-factor Portfolio Matrix, which matches business strength against market attractiveness to create a range of options, from additional investment in a product to its divestment.

Increasingly, innovation and new product development are the key to a successful product strategy. In some sectors, such as Pharmaceuticals, the investment needed to bring a new product to market is so great that companies need to generate significant sales over an extended period of time to recoup it. (See Case study 4.2)

maintain a sustainable competitive advantage. Its most recent major product launch, in 2009/10, was Victoza®, a treatment for type 2 diabetes, and the drug has already exceeded sales expectations in Europe, the US and Japan. Developing new products is a high-risk undertaking in the biopharmaceutical industry: to recoup the investment in the required research and development a company needs to be confident that its drug is likely to become a standard treatment. Companies also have to clear many regulatory hurdles to ensure that a drug is approved for use in different markets. Even after drugs are developed in the laboratory they have to be tested in small clinical trials and then with larger samples of patients and healthy volunteers before they can be licensed and gain regulatory approval from government agencies worldwide.

Victoza® competes directly with products made by Amylin Pharmaceuticals Inc. and Eli Lilly and Co. The launch confirms Novo Nordisk's position as the world leader in insulin-based products. The company also produces growth hormone products and drugs to combat haemophilia and other blood coagulation disorders. Novo Nordisk regards its products as differentiated (in terms of branding, product features, new ways of injecting insulin etc) from the generics that have come onto the market from emerging economies such as India and China, which are developing their own local pharmaceutical industries.

The international pharmaceutical market is growing almost twice as fast as established markets such as the US and Europe. For example, in India the market for insulin is growing at 20% a year and in China at over 30%. In the US growth is just 15% a year. Novo Nordisk has been aware of the likely growth of diabetes in emerging markets since the late 1990s. MadsOvlisen, the CEO in 1999, predicted a massive increase in diabetes in these markets over a 15-year period, based on observation of the same pattern of changing diets and sedentary lifestyles first identified in western economies being repeated in Asia.

Novo Nordisk has to balance the short-term demands of the investment community with the need to plan long-term product development. The company has a pipeline of products at different stages of development, which helps to maintain consistent sales and profits as patents run out on older products.

Service marketing plans – For many organisations tactics will also include the extended services marketing mix elements of People, Physical Evidence and Process. Awareness is growing that the service element of many customer value propositions is a key factor in purchase decisions and competitive advantage, with 'service-dominant logic' (Vargo and Lusch, 2004) a growing area of research.

Offerings such as fast-food and air travel have a significant service element, but even cars and large-scale industrial equipment will include service in the value proposition. Service contracts for maintenance can often bring in far more income over the life of the product than the capital outlay for the product itself.

Services have different characteristics from products in that they are:

- **Inseparable** – The service is consumed at the same time it is performed.
- **Intangible** – The service does not have physical substance.
- **Heterogeneous** – Standardisation is difficult because of the number of factors that influence service delivery (not least the people element).
- **Perishable** – Unlike products, services can't be stored.
- **Not ownable** – They are not physically owned by the customer.

This leads to a range of distinctive marketing issues that need to be accounted for in the mix part of the strategy.

QUICK QUIZ – CHECK YOUR KNOWLEDGE

Questions
1. What is the main difference between an organisation's mission and vision statements?
2. What does the acronym SMART stand for in relation to objectives?
3. Which is the highest-risk option in Ansoff's growth matrix?
4. What changes in the environment have led to the emergence of cost innovation strategies?

Answers
1. Vision is about aspiration and long-term direction; mission is about purpose and boundaries.
2. Specific, Measurable, Assignable, Realistic, Time-bound.
3. Diversification – both markets and products are new to the organisation so it might lack the capabilities and experience to succeed.
4. Emerging markets driving global demand, the downward pressure of global labour rates, global retailers pushing prices down.

FURTHER READING

Books
Core text:

Hooley, G., Nicoulaud, B., Piercy, N. and Rudd, J. (2017) *Marketing strategy and competitive positioning.* 6th edition. Harlow, FT Prentice Hall. Chapters 8-14.

Supplementary texts:

Aaker, D. and McLouglin, D. (2010) *Strategic market management: global perspectives*. Chichester, John Wiley. Chapters 7-14.

Cravens, D.W. and Piercy, N. (2012) *Strategic marketing*. 10th edition. US, McGraw-Hill. Chapters 6-13.

McDonald, M. and Wilson, H. (2016) *Marketing plans: how to prepare them, how to profit from them*. 8th edition. Chichester, John Wiley. Chapters 7-11.

References

Ansoff, I. (1988) *Corporate strategy*. London, Penguin.

Bowman, C. (2008) Generic strategies: a substitute for thinking? *360°. The Ashridge Journal*, Spring, pp6-11.

D'Aveni, R. (1994) *Hypercompetition: managing the dynamics of strategic maneuvering*. New York, The Free Press.

De Wit, B. and Meyer, R. (2010) *Strategy synthesis*. Andover, Cengage.

Elkington, J. (1999) *Cannibals with forks: the triple bottom line of 21st century business*. Oxford, Capstone.

Johnson, G., Whittington, R. and Scholes, K. (2011) *Exploring strategy*. Harlow, Prentice Hall.

Mintzberg, H. (1998) Generic strategies: toward a comprehensive framework. *In:* Lamb, R. and Shivastava, P. (eds.) *Advances in Strategic Management*. JAI Press.

Nicholson (1995) The MCC decision matrix: a tool for applying strategic logic to everyday activity. *Management Decision,* Vol33(6), pp4-10.

Porter, M. (1980) *Competitive strategy: techniques for analyzing industries and competitors*. New York, Free Press.

Rumelt, R. (1980) The evaluation of business strategy. *In:* Glueck, W., *Strategic management and business policy*. New York, McGraw-Hill.

Thompson, A., Strickland, L., Gamble, J., Peteraf, M., Janes, A. and Sutton, C. (2013) *Crafting and executing strategy: the quest for competitive advantage*. 1st European edition, Maidenhead, McGraw-Hill.

Vargo, S. and Lusch, R. (2004) Evolving to a new dominant logic for marketing. *Journal of Marketing*, Vol68(1), pp1-17.

Williamson, P. J. (2010) Cost innovation: preparing for a 'value-for-money' revolution. *Long Range Planning*, Vol43(2/3), pp343-353.

World Horse Welfare (2014) Our vision, mission and values. http://www.worldhorsewelfare.org/Our-vision-and-mission [accessed July 2014]

5.

IMPLEMENTATION AND CONTROL: MANAGING RESOURCES TO DELIVER THE STRATEGIC MARKETING PLAN

OUTLINE

This chapter will help you to manage resources to deliver the strategic marketing plan. At the end of the chapter you should be able to:

- Develop a realistic plan for the implementation of a marketing strategy.
- Determine the key variables and resources required to implement a successful marketing strategy.
- Identify and assess the risks, implications and issues involved in implementing a marketing strategy.

DEFINITIONS

Critical path – The set of tasks in a project that will take the longest time to complete.

Critical success factors (CSFs) – The competitive factors or activities that are needed to ensure the organisation succeeds.

Risk – An uncertainty factor that has the potential to harm an organisation.

Contingency planning – Preparing the organisation so it can respond to uncertain events.

5.1

Structure and content

McDonald and Wilson (2016) divide the marketing planning process into ten steps within four phases:

Phase one – Goal setting	1. Mission
	2. Corporate objectives
Phase two – Situation review	3. Marketing audit
	4. Market overview
	5. SWOT analysis
Phase three – Strategy formulation	6. Assumptions
	7. Marketing objectives and strategies
	8. Estimate expected results and identify alternative plans and mixes
Phase four – Resource allocation and monitoring	9. Budget
	10. First-year detailed implementation programme

Fig 5.1 The ten steps of the strategic marketing planning process *(Source: McDonald and Wilson, 2016, p57)*

The output of this process is the strategic marketing plan, which contains the following elements:

* Mission statement
* Financial summary
* Market overview
* SWOT analyses
* Assumptions
* Marketing objectives and strategies
* Three-year forecast and budgets

The implementation process itself covers four aspects, identified by Cravens and Piercy (2012) as:

* The activities to be implemented – mostly driven by the tactical mix elements of the plan
* How the implementation will be done
* The time and location of the implementation
* Who will be responsible for the implementation

There are a range of alternative formats and processes for producing plans, some of which, such as P.R. Smith's SOSTAC® model and the

APIC process, we mentioned in Chapter 1. Organisations and managers generally choose a template or framework that best fits their context.

Marketing organisation and team management

Cravens and Piercy (2013) offer this advice for marketers developing an implementation plan: "Since some of these characteristics [of evaluating organisation design] conflict with others, organisational design requires looking at priorities and balancing conflicting consequences."

The way marketing is organised depends on a number of factors. These may include the organisation's resources and capabilities, along with market and environmental forces. But the overall organisational structure and dominant corporate culture play a major role too, and marketers need to take account of this important factor when designing the marketing organisation and the implementation plan for the marketing strategy.

The various types of **organisational designs** include matrix, functional, product-focused and market-focused. Some organisations are designed along cross-functional lines, including GE, Honda and Harley-Davidson. These organisational forms will tend to dictate marketing organisational form, with the four archetypical **marketing organisational forms** being bureaucratic, transactional, organic and relational. For example, a traditional bureaucratic management can be less adaptive and therefore resistant to any radical departure from previous plans.

Marketers also need to think about the composition of the team and how centralised or decentralised it needs to be in order to implement the plan effectively. You should decide on the level of empowerment the team has as part of a wider rewards and incentives package: this will ensure that employees are sufficiently motivated and focused on the objectives in the strategy and other key performance indicators (we will cover these in detail in the next chapter).

Critical path analysis – managing the plan as a project

You will find many of the tools and techniques used for project management useful in helping you deliver the strategy effectively. Critical path analysis (CPA) is one of these. Also known as network analysis, it is frequently used to help plan and control large projects – including strategy implementation – which require a complete overview as well as the ability to focus on the fine detail. The critical path analysis technique helps you to divide the various components into smaller tasks, hold them in a logical sequence and estimate how long each will take. It helps to ensure that the project gets done in the minimum amount of time. You can also use this technique to help you allocate resources that will vary over the lifespan of the project. These might include the amount of labour or specialist equipment required at various points, for example.

In essence, a critical pathway includes the following:

1. A list of all activities required to complete the project.
2. The time (duration) that each activity will take to complete.
3. The dependencies between the activities.
4. Logical end points such as milestones or deliverables.

Based on this information, the CPA calculates the longest path of planned activities to logical end points, or to the end of the project, and the earliest and latest that each activity can start and finish without making the project longer. This process determines which activities are 'critical' (that is, on the longest path) and which have 'total float' (that is, can be delayed without making the project longer). In project management, a critical path is the sequence of project network activities that add up to the longest overall duration. This determines the shortest time possible it will take to complete the project. Any delay of an activity on the critical path directly affects the planned completion date for the project (there is no float on the critical path).

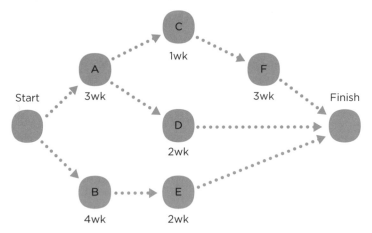

Fig 5.2 A typical critical path

More basic project tools, such as **Gantt Charts**, used for scheduling activities, and **Resource Histograms**, for planning resource requirements over the period of the plan, can also prove useful in managing the execution of a strategy. These and many other templates and frameworks are now available in a variety of software packages.

Agile project management
Agile techniques offer an alternative to traditional project management. Rather than trying to control and map out the entire project in all its complexity, this system breaks work down into much smaller pieces,

each lasting between two and four weeks. Agile project management also splits the role of the project manager among different team members. In addition to the (shared) project manager role, there are two other distinct positions in an Agile team:

- Product owner – who sets project goals and priorities.
- Scrum master – who works with the team to prioritise the individual tasks and acts as a troubleshooter.

Teams are largely self-managing and responsible for reporting progress on a regular basis.

Agile project management was originally developed by software engineers to help manage large IT and coding projects. As marketing moves more into the digital arena this more iterative form of project development with short cycles and strong links to continuous improvement methodologies is becoming increasingly attractive. (We cover this in more detail in Chapter 6.) Using Agile techniques for implementing the marketing strategy gives marketers a good deal of flexibility to respond to changes in the market.

Action priority matrix

As the marketing plan is put into action, changes will inevitably occur to make some aspects of the plan redundant and other elements more significant. In some cases you won't be able to complete all the proposed activities within the planned time-frame. You might need to shift some of what you planned for the first year of the three-year strategy to a later date or even drop it altogether, for example. The Action Priority Matrix (see Figure 5.3 overleaf) is a useful tool for helping managers to prioritise their work. It assesses activities in terms of their impact on key objectives and the effort needed to achieve the desired outcome, allowing you to easily identify and prioritise in the implementation plan those activities that will deliver the greatest impact for the least effort.

ACTIVITY 5.1

Make a list of the activities you are currently working on and then score each of them for impact and effort (with 1 as the lowest and 10 the highest). Then plot them on an Action Priority matrix.

Legislative, regulatory and code of conduct considerations

Implementation plans also need to take into account a range of internal and external factors over which marketers may have little or no influence. For example, those working for organisations operating on a multinational basis will need to consider a wide array of local and regional legislation and regulation that can affect everything from packaging to promotional techniques. UK and US laws designed to prevent bribery and corruption have force in foreign countries too, and can have an impact on events and hospitality elements of business that have traditionally played a significant role in B2B sales and marketing. Marketers also need to be mindful of the standards of behaviour and actions set by their own organisations, as well as CIM's code of conduct. One of CIM's objectives in its Royal Charter is "to promote and maintain high standards of professional skill, ability and integrity among persons engaged in marketing products and services." (CIM, 2012)

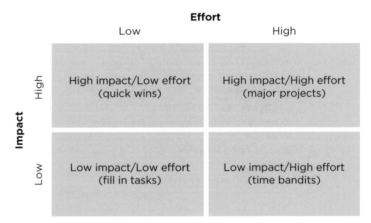

Figure 5.3 Action Priority Matrix

5.2

Critical success factors

Critical success factors (CSFs), as the name suggests, are factors that are essential for success in a particular market or industry. They might be product attributes, for example, or particular marketing resources and capabilities – such as access to distribution channels or ownership of patents. CSFs will vary between industries and markets so you need to understand the context of the organisation in order to identify the appropriate CSFs. To do this you need to understand:

- The basis on which customers choose between rival products and services. What elements of the customer value proposition are essential in meeting their needs?
- The assets and abilities the organisation needs to be successful in its industry or market. These can be determined by looking at the winners and losers in the sector.
- The weaknesses that may put an organisation at a competitive disadvantage.

Having already carried out an effective analysis of the internal and external environments, managers should have this sort of information in mind as they set the objectives for the strategic marketing plan. CSFs are closely related to Key Performance Indicators (KPIs), which we will look at in more detail in the next chapter.

Resource requirements

The final phase of developing the marketing strategy should be to state clearly what resources the plan needs in order to be successfully implemented. The asset categories we covered in Chapters 2 and 3 provide a menu of possible requirements. Financial resources, in the form of a budget, are the most obvious element, but the plan might also need human resources – expertise in social media or mobile marketing for example – or organisational systems such as customer relationship management software.

Organisational culture

In Chapter 2 we looked at culture as a potential source of competitive advantage for the organisation. Instilling a culture that supports the implementation of the strategy is important because it can result in a more flexible and responsive organisation whose employees need less supervision and can act independently. Managers can be confident that teams will focus on the relevant activities and measures. However, culture can also be a barrier to effective implementation – especially if the strategy being executed represents a radical change from the past. For this reason, strategic marketing plans also need to cover internal marketing, which can help capture the hearts and minds of employees.

McKinsey 7-S Framework – configuring the whole organisation to support strategic implementation

McKinsey's 7-S Framework model (Waterman *et al*, 1980), named after the consulting firm McKinsey & Co which developed it, encompasses all the elements of organisation design and how they fit together. The elements covered by the McKinsey's 7-S framework are strategy, structure, systems, staff, style, skills and superordinate goals (or shared values in an earlier version).

- **Strategy** – Encompasses the overall position of the organisation and its long-term direction.
- **Structure** – Defines the formal roles of employees within the strategy, including their responsibilities and reporting lines. The main structural forms include matrix, multidivisional and functional.
- **Systems** – The various formal and informal processes that rule and support people inside and outside an organisation. These include budgeting systems, marketing information systems, training systems, cost accounting procedures, etc, which support the day-to-day running of the organisations
- **Staff** – The different types of people within the organisation, and the systems of reward, recruitment and socialisation used to develop them. Organisations need the right people for the strategy they are following, and, particularly where the organisation structure is being altered, it is vital that department heads have the appropriate abilities.
- **Style** – An organisation's leadership style can take various forms, including autocratic, participative, collaborative and coercive. It is signalled by how the top managers spend their time, and their symbolic behaviour. Leadership style needs to fit well with the culture of the organisation – so for example, a participative or collaborative style is much more likely to achieve results in a matrix structure organisation
- **Skills** – Employees' talents should be developed into the capabilities required by the organisational strategy through training, improved information technology and rewards.
- **Superordinate goals (or shared values)** – Are the goals that form the overall purpose of the organisation and drive it forward. They encompass its vision, values and objectives.

McKinsey's 7-S framework draws attention to at least three organisational features.

1. It shows that every one of the 7-S elements has many aspects and highlights how all these aspects need to fit together. There is more to organising than simply getting the correct structure.
2. The framework also shows that if one of the main elements is changed then the other elements will have to be changed as well in order to preserve the correct alignment.
3. Changing single elements is likely to cause disruption until the point that the other elements are aligned accordingly.

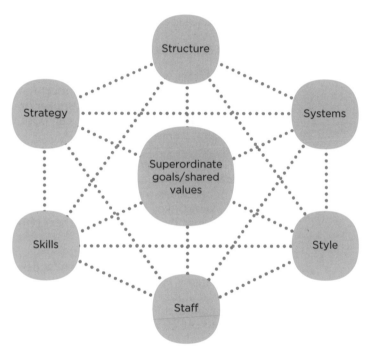

Fig 5.4 McKinsey's 7 S Framework

5.3

RISKS AND ISSUES ARISING FROM IMPLEMENTATION

Any major undertaking, including a project or the execution of a strategy, involves risk, and the implementation plan and the team delivering it need to take this into account. Some risks will be uncontrollable events in the external environment whereas others may arise from the internal politics that are common in all but the smallest organisations. This section provides marketers with a set of tools to prepare for unexpected and unwelcome events.

Risk assessment

Risk assessment or risk management pinpoints the risks contained within the overview of a project or plan and determines what might go wrong and the likely consequences.

Risks can be divided into six categories:

- **Political** – Either within an organisation, such as a change of CEO or the level of senior management support for the strategy, or outside it, such as the defection of a key supplier or distributor to a rival.
- **Social** – Media or pressure groups can pose risks to a strategy in some circumstances.
- **Physical** – Issues such as distribution resources or plant, equipment and buildings being affected by disasters such as fire.
- **Technical** – Systems failures, such as ecommerce websites or customer relationship management systems.
- **Labour** – Loss of key staff as a result of illness or death.
- **Legal** – Actions by customers or other connected stakeholders to seek redress through the courts.

Once you've identified sources of potential risk, you can then ask the following questions. How likely is it that this risk will show itself? Can we control or limit it in any way? What will happen if this risk occurs? How can we control it in the least damaging way? Different strategies of dealing with risk can be summed up as follows:

- Avoidance (eliminate, or not become involved).
- Reduction (optimise, limit, mitigate).
- Sharing (transfer – outsource to third party or insure).
- Retention (accept, plan on dealing with any incidence and budget accordingly).

When you've assessed the likelihood of any risk occurring (and an 'impact/probability matrix' can help you here – see Fig 5.5) you can develop a contingency plan to manage the potential risk. You need to make all the stakeholders associated with the project aware of this process in order to cover off every angle.

Impact	Probability		
	High	Medium	Low
High	Critical	Critical	Significant
Medium	Significant	Significant	Minor
Low	Minor	Minor	Insignificant

Fig 5.5 Impact/probability matrix

Contingency planning

Any strategic implementation plan should contain contingency plans – that is, activities to deal with events that may be unlikely, but which could have a big impact. Each of the major risks identified using the impact/probability matrix will need a contingency plan covering the following elements:

- A series of activities and milestones designed to bring the strategy back on track.
- Key personnel who need to be involved, with clear details of their role and responsibilities.
- Details of how the plan will be tested.
- Coverage of any additional training staff may need (presenting to the media, for example).
- Details of how the plan will be updated as the risk it is designed to mitigate changes.

General Motors in South Africa

In 2013, a month-long strike by the National Union of Metalworkers in South Africa (NUMSA) in the automotive sector cost car manufacturers in the country over £1.2 billion in lost sales. The South African operation of General Motors (GM) developed contingency plans to avoid a repeat of the losses. The plans were designed to ensure that it always had at least two weeks' worth of finished cars and trucks in stock, and that potential alternative components and materials suppliers were available in case it had to close production at its main plant. In July 2014 NUMSA members went on strike again – and while GM had to stop production at its main plant, the stockpiles that it had developed as part of its contingency plan helped to mitigate the damage to its sales.

(Source: BBC News, 2014)

Stakeholder analysis

One of the biggest risks facing marketers trying to execute a strategy is politics inside and outside the organisation. Powerful stakeholders can derail even the best crafted strategy. Marketers need to be able to identify their stakeholders correctly in order to understand what they expect from the organisation, and then formulate a strategy for managing relationships with them. You should start by categorising your stakeholders, and we looked at one framework for doing this, the Seven Markets model, in Chapter 1. Alternatively, you could use the following classifications: economic stakeholders, social/political stakeholders, technological stakeholders and community stakeholders. Different stakeholder groups will have different views on how the organisation should be run and different success criteria.

Stakeholder influence can be demonstrated by stakeholder mapping using the power/interest matrix (Mendelow, 1991). See Fig 5.6 opposite. The matrix shows the expectations and power of stakeholders and gives marketers an indication of political priorities. It's important to understand how much power each stakeholder holds in terms of their ability to influence an organisation's strategy, and the extent to which they are prepared to wield that power in order to have their interests and views recognised and taken into account.

The amount and type of power that each stakeholder group has varies widely. They might have specific knowledge, control valuable resources or have an important set of connections, for example. Their respective interests also vary, depending on their views generally and how they perceive the organisation's place in the market.

Level of interest

	Low	High
Power Low	Minimal effort	Keep informed
Power High	Keep satisfied	Key players

Figure 5.6 Power/interest matrix *(Source: Mendelow, 1991)*

Unless marketers understand the interests, power and potential impact of each stakeholder group, there could be dire consequences for the organisation as a whole. Stakeholder analysis can help here. By applying the power/interest matrix, or similar techniques such as that outlined in the work by Mitchell *et al* (1997) on 'stakeholder salience', managers can develop different engagement strategies for the various groups of stakeholders based on a logical approach rather than reacting to those who 'shout loudest'. The Real Life case below illustrates this issue.

Manchester United's stakeholders

English premier league football club Manchester United is no stranger to the politics of strategy and the effect this can have on the choices managers and owners make. The club was controversially acquired in 2005 by the Glazer family in a leveraged buyout that was unpopular with many of its fans. Fig 5.7 below shows the range of stakeholders the club had at the point it was taken over. Fig 5.8 then illustrates the key players – those stakeholders the Glazer family needed to keep onside in order to ensure their takeover plan succeeded.

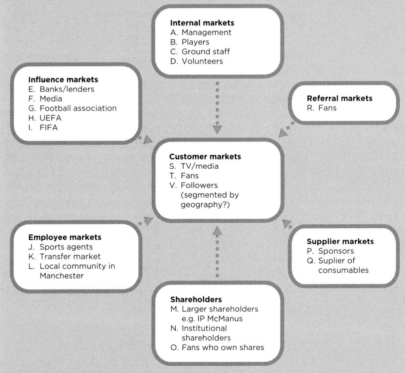

Internal markets
A. Management
B. Players
C. Ground staff
D. Volunteers

Influence markets
E. Banks/lenders
F. Media
G. Football association
H. UEFA
I. FIFA

Referral markets
R. Fans

Customer markets
S. TV/media
T. Fans
V. Followers
   (segmented by
   geography?)

Employee markets
J. Sports agents
K. Transfer market
L. Local community in
   Manchester

Supplier markets
P. Sponsors
Q. Suplier of
   consumables

Shareholders
M. Larger shareholders
   e.g. IP McManus
N. Institutional
   shareholders
O. Fans who own shares

Fig 5.7 Seven Markets model applied to Manchester United stakeholders

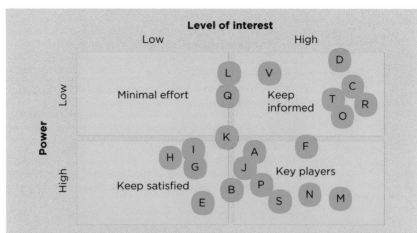

Fig 5.8 Power/interest matrix applied to Manchester United stakeholders

From Fig 5.7 and 5.8 we can see that institutional shareholders and owners of large numbers of shares, such as JP McManus, were the groups the Glazer family needed to engage with more closely, through face-to-face meetings, phone calls, regular briefings and so on. Other key players they needed to engage with on an intensive basis were the club's management, the players, sponsors, TV and media companies, and sports agents. The power of these stakeholders typically stemmed from the large amount of income they brought to the club or, in the case of star players, their control of rare assets. The 'loudest' stakeholder groups were undoubtedly the fans and followers, many of whom were very interested in the outcome of the takeover and made their views known through protests and, in some cases, violent attacks on the police and vehicles thought to be carrying the Glazer family. However, their level of power was judged low – so the engagement strategy was simply to keep them informed, along with other stakeholders, through press releases and news items on the club's website and via newsletters and match-day programmes.

Managing change

Managing change effectively is, in practice, a rare skill among managers. Poor results ensue, and this has an adverse effect on employees' morale and can make them resistant to the changes imposed. However, thorough planning and preparation, combined with clear communication, increases the likelihood that the change will be successful and that employees accept and even welcome it.

There are many causes of, or reasons for, change. The organisation might need to alter products or services to meet new customer requirements, for example, or new legislation could require changes to advertising or improvements in quality. Technological advances could mean changes have to be made in order to maintain a competitive edge. The organisation may have decided to re-brand or make changes to an existing brand. Changes to professional qualifications and advances in marketing skills and knowledge indicate that organisational change is required.

While some of these changes can be self-imposed, others are forced on the organisation from the outside, which can affect the way change is structured and managed. Timescales outside the organisation's power also have an impact. Careful planning is required in order to avoid pitfalls when reorganising tasks, activities and departments.

There are a number of practical tools that a marketer can use to help manage the kind of changes involved in executing a strategy. For example, Balogun et al's (1998) Change Kaleidoscope (see Fig 5.9) is a useful guide to the contextual issues to be considered and the design choices available.

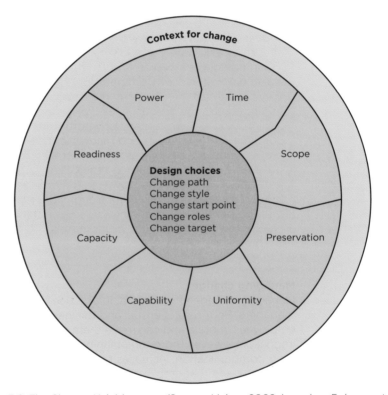

Fig 5.9 The Change Kaleidoscope *(Source: Mabey, 2002; based on Balogun et al, 1998)*

To understand the context of the change marketers need to think about the following aspects:

- **Time** – The degree of urgency and the timing of the change.
- **Scope** – The extent of the change – how wide will it reach and is it likely to be incremental or transformational?
- **Preservation** – What needs to be kept from the existing situation?
- **Uniformity** – How similar or different are the groups that will be involved in and affected by the change, and how differentiated should your approach therefore be?
- **Capability** – Does the organisation have the skills and abilities needed to ensure the change is successful?
- **Capacity** – Does it have the resources needed?
- **Readiness** – Have the organisation and the teams involved in the change recognised that this is necessary or will the change need to be imposed?
- **Power** – Does the person leading the change have the authority to ensure the change is followed through?

Marketers can then design the change process by evaluating the following choices in the light of the context:

- **Change path** – Where should the change be located on the continuum between revolutionary and evolutionary?
- **Change style** – Should the change be top down and imposed or is there scope for an 'action learning' approach with mostly bottom-up initiatives?
- **Change start point** – Where should the change process start within the organisation – with a project team, senior managers, or with an entirely new team?
- **Change roles** – Who will begin the change process, who will lead or manage it and who will put the change programme into action?
- **Change target** – What is being changed? Is it products, processes, skills, systems, structures, culture, or a combination of all these elements?

Prescriptions for change
Other models of managing major changes give more of a step-by-step approach. John Kotter's (1995) framework is a typical example:

1. Establish a sense of urgency.
2. Create the guiding coalition.
3. Develop a vision and strategy.
4. Communicate the change vision.
5. Empower broad-based action.
6. Generate short-term wins.
7. Consolidate gains and produce more change.
8. Anchor new approaches in the culture.

However, as we have seen from looking at stakeholders and other issues around implementing strategies, a one-size-fits-all approach won't work in all contexts. Knowing why different groups and individuals respond to change in a particular way can be extremely valuable for a manager leading the execution of a strategic marketing plan.

Recent work by Sheard *et al* (2009) suggests that looking behind the actions of managers is the key to understanding their motivations. Fig 5.9 below illustrates how the degree of involvement with a change management programme, along with managers' feelings about that programme can give rise to a set of different political behaviours.

Fig 5.9 Political behaviours *(Source: Sheard et al, 2009)*

QUICK QUIZ – CHECK YOUR KNOWLEDGE

Questions
1. What are the four phases of the marketing planning process?
2. What are the four main ways of dealing with risk?
3. What is contingency planning?
4. Why is it important to understand the levels of power and interest of different stakeholder groups?

Answers
1. Goal setting, situation review, strategy formulation, and resource allocation and monitoring.
2. Avoidance, reduction, sharing, retention.
3. Preparing the organisation so it can respond to uncertain events. This is usually achieved by having a series of action plans that are implemented in response to or triggered by particular events. Contingency plans are a way of future-proofing a strategy,

because they force managers to think about a series of 'what if?' questions – for example, what if our website is hacked? What if our CRM systems crashes? What if the TV advert our agency produces is banned by regulators?

4. Because this will help determine the communications objectives and mix for different groups. It is important to adopt a segmented approach to working with stakeholders and to do this you need to be able to identify and assess the groups in a logical manner. Otherwise you may focus on the wrong groups, which could have an impact on your ability to execute your chosen strategy.

FURTHER READING

Books

Core text:

Hooley, G., Nicoulaud, B., Piercy, N. and Rudd, J. (2017) *Marketing strategy and competitive positioning*. 6th edition. Harlow, FT Prentice Hall. Chapters 15-17.

Supplementary texts:

Aaker, D. and McLouglin, D. (2010) *Strategic market management: global perspectives*. Chichester, John Wiley. Chapter 15.

Cravens, D.W. and Piercy, N. (2012) *Strategic marketing*. 10th edition. US, McGraw-Hill. Chapter 15.

McDonald, M. and Wilson, H. (2016) *Marketing plans: how to prepare them, how to profit from them*. Chichester, John Wiley. Chapter 12

References

Balogun, J., Hope Hailey, V., Johnson, G. and Scholes, K. (1998) *Exploring strategic change*. Harlow, Prentice Hall.

BBC News (2014) General Motors South Africa closes plant due to strike. *BBC News online,* 4 July. http://www.bbc.co.uk/news/business-28157615 [accessed July 2014]

Christopher, M., Payne, A. and Ballantyne, D. (2002) *Relationship marketing: creating stakeholder value*. Oxford, Butterworth-Heinemann.

CIM (2012) *Code of professional standards*. Cookham, CIM. http://www.cim.co.uk/Files/codeofprofessionalstandards10.pdf [accessed July 2014]

Kotter, J. (1995) Leading change: why transformation efforts fail. *Harvard Business Review*, Vol73(2), pp53-67.

Mabey, C. (2002) *Preparing for change*. Milton Keynes, The Open University.

Mendelow, A. (1991) Stakeholder mapping. *Proceedings of the 2nd International Conference on Information Systems*, Cambridge MA.

Mitchell, R., Agle, B. and Wood, D. (1997) Toward a theory of stakeholder identification and salience: defining the principle of who and what really counts. *Academy of Management Review*, Vol22(4), pp853-886.

Rothman, J. (1998) Action evaluation and conflict resolution in theory and practice. *Mediation Journal,* Vol15(2), pp119-131.

Sheard, G, Kakabadse, A, and Kakabadse, N. (2009) Organisational politics: the shadow side of leadership. *Proceedings of the European Conference on Management, Leadership and Governance*, pp232-241.

6.

IMPLEMENTATION AND CONTROL: MONITOR, MEASURE AND ADAPT THE MARKETING PLAN TO DRIVE CONTINUOUS IMPROVEMENT

OUTLINE

This chapter will help you to monitor, measure and adapt the marketing plan in order to continuously improve it. At the end of this chapter you will be able to:

- Recommend appropriate control mechanisms to measure and monitor the progress of the implemented marketing strategy.
- Understand the importance of continuous improvement in relation to marketing strategy and planning.
- Create an effective continuous improvement plan.

DEFINITIONS

Shareholder Value Added (SVA) – "A framework for evaluating options for improving shareholder value by determining the trade-offs between reinvesting in existing businesses, investing in new businesses and returning cash to stockholders." *(McDonald and Wilson, 2016)*

Marketing dashboard – A report or software tool that presents key marketing metrics and data in an easily accessible format.

Key Performance Indicators (KPIs) – The critical measures of success for an organisation.

Strategic drift – "The tendency for strategies to develop incrementally on the basis of historical and cultural influences, but fail to keep pace with a changing environment." *(Johnson et al, 2011)*

Total Quality Management (TQM) – "Entails creating a total quality culture bent on continuously improving the performance of every task and value chain activity." (Thompson *et al*, 2013)

Six Sigma – A continuous improvement system that uses advanced statistical techniques to reduce errors and variability in business processes.

Kaizen – A Japanese philosophy underpinning continuous improvement to business processes.

6.1

MEASURING, MONITORING AND CONTROLLING THE IMPLEMENTATION OF MARKETING STRATEGY

Strategic marketing plans will often require substantial financial resources, so it is natural that any organisation will want to measure the outputs from the plan against what was promised or forecast. Measurement and monitoring are done at a number of levels, using a variety of metrics, and in this section we will cover some of these measures and look at how you can use them to control the plan.

Finance measures/control ratios

In Chapter 2 we introduced some of the key ratios and measures for understanding the strength of an organisation's financial resources. These measures usually form part of the marketing audit and provide a baseline from which to generate strategic and financial objectives. This makes them a key element in the measurement and control of the marketing strategy too. Therefore, we can use them to measure the success of a strategy or the value it adds in the long term. According to McDonald and Wilson (2016) we can measure 'value added' in four ways:

- **Value-chain analysis** – looking at costs and outputs in comparison with competitors.
- **Shareholder value added (SVA)** – which is calculated by subtracting the net capital employed multiplied by the cost of capital (expressed as a percentage) from profit after tax. This measures the organisation's ability to earn more than its total cost of capital.
- **Customer value** – looking at measures such as customer satisfaction and loyalty.
- **Accounting value** – the results and ratios from the annual accounts and quarterly updates.

Marketers need to be clear about which financial ratios the marketing strategy supports and ensure that they review these measures regularly as part of their monitoring of the plan. The investment in marketing can be substantial in competitive environments and financial stakeholders – especially investors – will want to be assured that the funds are being used effectively and are delivering the desired returns. In particular, revenues for the business are likely to come under scrutiny. One of the main challenges marketers face is linking their activity explicitly to increases (or decreases) in sales. What they can do more easily, however, is measure the effectiveness of the strategies and tactics in the plan using operational indicators (which we cover in the next section).

The other financial element of the strategy that marketers need to focus on is the budget. The budget for the strategic marketing plan will incorporate a forecast of income and expenditure which, like any financial estimate, needs to be used to monitor and measure the progress of the plan. Marketers face a number of challenges in constructing the budget – especially if the markets they are serving are dynamic and changing rapidly. Marketers need to produce regular variance reports looking at planned expenditure against actual expenditure, and if the difference between the two is above a certain level (for example + or – 10%) they will need to explain the variance and take action to address it.

Operational measures

Marketing measures should give an indication of the impact the tactics in the marketing mix are having and whether they are achieving the desired level of competitive advantage in the market. There is a wide range of metrics to consider here. However, the choice will be influenced by the objectives set in the strategic marketing plan and the availability of data. Potential operational measures can be divided into a number of categories (Cravens and Piercy, 2012):

Category	Examples
Competitive and customer metrics	Market share, consumer purchase intentions, customer loyalty, willingness to recommend.
Profitability metrics	Break-even sales level, contribution margins.
Product and portfolio metrics	Market penetration, sales volumes for new products vs existing products, repeat purchases.
Customer profitability metrics	Customer lifetime value, acquisition and retention costs.
Sales and channel metrics	Percentage of outlets stocking the product, inventory turnover.
Pricing metrics	Proportion of customers considering product good value, competitors' response to price changes.
Promotion metrics	Coupon redemption rates, baseline vs incremental sales.
Advertising, media and web metrics	Opportunities to view, cost-per-thousand impressions, share of voice, cost per click.
Financial metrics	In addition to the measures in Chapter 2, payback period, return on marketing investment.
Brand equity metrics	Familiarity relative to other brands, brand preference.

| Innovation metrics | Number of innovations launched, percentage of revenue from launches in past three years. |
| Internal market metrics | Awareness of corporate goals, customer brand empathy. |

Fig 6.1 Operational measures for marketing *(Source: Cravens and Piercy, 2012 – based on Ferris et al, 2006)*

KPIs and critical success factors

As we have seen, marketers are likely to be dealing with a large number and wide range of measures and performance indicators. These are covered in more detail in the other compulsory module at this level, Mastering Metrics. A strategic marketing plan has to focus on those measures that affect the organisation's ability to survive and prosper.

Key Performance Indicators (KPIs) are used to measure the critical success factors (CSFs) that underpin the objectives in a strategic marketing plan. CSFs are factors that are essential for success in a particular market or industry, and might include product attributes and particular marketing resources and capabilities – such as access to distribution channels or ownership of patents. CSFs will vary between industries and markets so it is important to understand the context of the organisation for which the factors are being established. In order to identify CSFs for a particular market or industry marketers need to understand the following:

- The basis on which customers choose between rival products and services – what elements of the customer value proposition are essential in meeting their needs?
- The assets and abilities an organisation needs to be successful in its industry or market. This can be determined by looking at the winners and losers in the sector.
- The weaknesses that will put an organisation at a competitive disadvantage.

You should have this sort of information at your fingertips as a result of your analysis of the internal and external environments, and you need to keep it in mind as you set the objectives for the strategic marketing plan. You should allocate a specific measure or KPI to each CSF and monitor these to ensure that this element of the plan is on track and that the related objectives will be met.

There will only be a limited number of factors that are truly critical to an organisation's success, so it is important not to have too many KPIs. Parmenter (2007) suggests that organisations should have no more than ten KPIs used in combination with a further 80 performance indicators and ten 'key result indicators'. However, balanced scorecard approaches (Kaplan and Norton, 1992) often produce significantly more KPIs – up to 20 – as the scorecard covers between four and six areas of the business (financial, customer, learning and innovation, and internal operations were the original areas included in this framework).

ACTIVITY 6.1

Choose two organisations – one should be a government or not-for-profit organisation and the other a commercial enterprise. Compile a list of KPIs/CSFs for each organisation (either by looking them up from organisational sources or by imagining what measures would be most important for each organisation). How do the lists differ?

Time intervals required on control measures

In the past, strategic objectives have been reviewed on a quarterly, annual or even biennial basis depending on the context of the organisation. As the rate of change in some markets increases and the access to real-time performance data on grows, it is possible, and in some cases desirable, to monitor control measures on a much more frequent basis. As an example of the speed sometimes needed in e-marketing contexts, Chaffey and Smith (2013) point to the incident when the twitter feed of fast-food chain McDonald's was hacked and the company responded within an hour of the attack.

However, monitoring some strategic metrics and activities on a frequent basis can be counter-productive and take up large amounts of valuable management time for little return. So marketers need to take a balanced approach to this activity. You'll need to monitor operational measures fairly frequently so as to keep the project and processes on track. But compared with other business functions, such as production, it can take longer for changes to marketing processes and activities to produce tangible or quantifiable results. For example, changing content on a website might produce instant results in terms of visits or mentions on social media, but the impact on sales could take much longer to come through.

Marketing dashboards

Accurate measurement of marketing performance is essential in order to correctly assess current and future marketing activities. The marketing dashboard, which has become an increasingly important tool for senior managers, allows you to control, measure and monitor short-term activities as well as plan for the longer term. It's no accident that it's named after the central control panel of a car: the marketing dashboard shows key performance data in an immediately understandable way. Once senior management has agreed and approved the parameters of key marketing metrics, marketers can evaluate and communicate marketing performance from the data presented on the marketing dashboard.

Advanced computer software packages are available to facilitate both the input and interpretation of key marketing data. But the role of the human being is important in interpreting such data and making decisions that take account of the real results achieved compared with the anticipated ones.

ACTIVITY 6.2

Using a selection of measures from Fig 6.1 above – or from your own research into the topic – construct a marketing dashboard template for key marketing metrics in your organisation, or one you know well. Think about how this will link to the organisation's objectives.

CONTINUOUS IMPROVEMENT

Monitoring performance on a regular basis can allow an organisation to make incremental changes to its strategy in response to changes in the environment. As customers become more demanding and have greater choice and additional access to knowledge due to increasing globalisation and technological advances such as the internet, being able to make incremental changes to different aspects of the marketing strategy and mix elements can give an organisation an advantage over its rivals.

Strategic drift

Even in relatively stable markets the external environment changes over time and an organisation's strategy will often change in an incremental way to keep pace. Such changes will often be driven by routines and processes built up over time – for example, organisational knowledge of how to respond to a particular change in the environment. A restaurant chain, for instance, will respond to changes in customers' food preferences by regularly designing new menus. However, when there is a more dramatic or discontinuous change in the environment (see McGahan's Industry Trajectories of Change matrix, covered in Chapter 3 – Fig 3.4) or the organisation's strategy doesn't keep pace with the changes in the external environment, then strategic drift occurs. In other words, the environment continues to change but the organisation's strategy doesn't change fast enough to keep pace with it. This might be as a result of the core rigidities and sticky resources we discussed in Chapter 2. Eventually, if the environment continues to change, the organisation's financial performance will decline, at which point management might try new approaches or develop a new strategy. If this doesn't turn the company around, it will ultimately go out of business or be acquired by another firm.

Strategic drift demonstrates the importance of maintaining a high level of continuous improvement in order to keep pace with changes in the external environment.

Total quality management

In their bid for operating excellence many organisations rely on total quality management (TQM) as one of their most potent process management tools. TQM is a management philosophy that advocates and encourages excellence across the whole of an organisation's enterprises and in every department. It also emphasises continuous improvement in all operations.

The two main strands are focusing on producing quality goods and meeting high customer satisfaction standards. But to achieve greater success in all areas of its operation the organisation has to extend this philosophy to every department, even if those departments have little or no direct involvement with the final product. Management has to motivate everyone in the organisation to find ways to improve every aspect of their products and/or services. But they also have to be patient, as it takes at least six months before TQM delivers any real benefit. From a marketing perspective TQM's focus on the quality of the product or service and customer satisfaction is in line with the discipline's fundamental rationale. It also provides a lever for helping to build the all-important customer orientation.

CASE STUDY 6.1
Jessops falls prey to strategic drift

One of the UK high street's best known stores, camera retailer Jessops, went into administration in January 2013. The firm was founded in 1935 and had built up a strong brand due to its reputation for customer service and prime locations in most major towns and cities. The chain controlled 192 shops and employed over 2,000 people in the UK. Jessops' decline is a good example of strategic drift and its impact on an organisation. Competition from supermarkets, and then internet retailers, had started to affect its performance and in 2009 the company narrowly avoided bankruptcy by striking a deal with its main lender HSBC. Jessops had not responded effectively to the changes in the market, believing that its high level of customer service and knowledgeable staff would continue to give it a competitive advantage once the recession ended.

But the biggest blow for the firm was the growth of smartphone ownership and the quality of the built-in cameras they contained. This meant that the amateur market, which had provided much of Jessops' revenue, stopped buying separate cameras. Increasing online choice and niche, specialist camera websites with much larger ranges of equipment had already lured away many of the professional customers. This dramatic decline in Jessops' traditional customer base reduced revenues to an unsustainably low level.

(Source: BBC News, 2013)

Kaizen theory
Kaizen – a process of making continual incremental improvements to business processes – originated in Japan as a response to the work of Deming (see section on Plan, Do, Check, Act below) and Juran. The reasoning behind this philosophy is that it's always possible to enhance the operations of the company and that employees should therefore be encouraged to look for ways to solve even minor operational problems and deliver improvements. In many organisations Kaizen is synonymous with small groups working to improve products and processes through Quality Circles and Work Improvement Teams. Strategic marketing

plans need to acknowledge that incremental and emergent change (change that is chaotic and less controlled than planned change)may be necessary to keep pace with continuously evolving markets and customer behaviour. Most organisational attention is focused on the kind of dramatic innovations that could revolutionise their markets, but making small improvements can yield big returns. Recent research (Bolton *et al*, 2014) has shown that in service encounters there are three key approaches to enhancing a customer's experience of consuming of a service:

- Holistic service design, including providing human touchpoints.
- Designing services that deliver emotionally engaging experiences.
- Integrating human touch and emotional engagement in service encounters with customers.

Real Life 6.1 below illustrates how one organisation approached this through using real-time customer data. By designing continuous improvement principles into the marketing strategy, managers allow front-line staff to be responsive to customers and make changes to the way a service is delivered.

REAL LIFE 6.1

Harrah's Hotels

Harrah's, part of the Caesars Entertainment Corporation, is a US-based company running resort hotels and casinos. Its customer relationship management (CRM) programme uses continuous improvement principles to produce enhanced rewards for customers. Unlike typical service loyalty programmes, which are rarely tailored to the individual, Harrah's recognises that customers have personal preferences that may be very different from each other. By monitoring customer activity, the company's customer service teams are able to customise the CRM tools in real time so that they can offer customers relevant rewards depending on their habits and behaviour.

(Source: Bolton et al, 2014)

Other techniques that support continuous improvement strategies include Six Sigma and Lean Management. The techniques are different but the intended outcomes are similar in that the end goal is to improve the quality of the product or service and customer satisfaction. From being a commercially driven discipline, continuous improvement techniques have now moved into many organisations in the public and not-for-profit sectors, including schools, charities, government departments and local councils.

6.3

Plan, Do, Check, Act

At its most basic, continuous improvement involves a four-stage approach best illustrated by the 'Deming cycle' (see Fig 6.2 below). This is based on a 'plan, do, check, act' pattern.

- **Plan** – Clarifies who is involved, the purpose of the project, what needs to be changed, the data available and how this data will be used.
- **Do** – Based on the plan, a small change is made.
- **Check** – The outcome of the change is then monitored.
- **Act** – The results of the study are applied to generate improvements in performance and used to inform future decisions.

Figure 6.2 Deming's PDCA cycle

Benchmarking is one source of ideas for changing the organisation and its processes. Being able to compare itself with leading performers allows an organisation to improve, adapt and sustain its own ideas, practices and ways of operating. Various benchmarking methods have evolved to help firms judge performance standards, best practice and competitive analysis.

Deciding on who or what should be the benchmark, and what process to scrutinise, is the first part or 'planning' stage. The 'doing' stage needs both direct contact with the benchmark organisation and research to discover secondary data to help identify the standards and actions that may be needed. When this research is 'checked' or analysed, gaps in performance and the reasons for them can be identified. The final 'act' part of the process involves applying the new information and any lessons learned to improve or exceed performance standards.

Action learning

Action learning was originally developed by Cambridge academic Professor Reg Revans. This tool encourages users to reflect on their own knowledge of a subject and to use questioning to generate insights into a particular topic. Organisations will often use action learning Sets, teams of eight to ten individuals, to tackle difficult and intractable problems through questioning. The insights generated by this technique are then used to create action plans. There are parallels with Deming's work, although a very separate culture and set of practitioners has grown up around Revans's work.

Data collection plans

An important part of the planning element of continuous improvement is deciding what data to collect and how to collect it. We covered the main options for collecting data and information in Chapter 3. Much of the information collected via research methods and gathered through market intelligence channels will be useful here. The case study below illustrates how the plan for collecting data drove the rest of the customer satisfaction improvement process at Heathrow airport.

CASE STUDY 6.2

BAA: transforming customer satisfaction at Heathrow

In 2007 Heathrow airport had a major problem with customer satisfaction. In a benchmarking exercise with other European airports it was ranked 13th out of 13. In order to improve the situation the management team decided to look in detail at the processes using Lean/Six Sigma principles – in other words, they put the customer at the heart of their plan to redesign airport processes. They developed plans to collect data on four different aspects of the airport's operations that directly affected customers. By looking at how passengers, baggage, planes and cargo moved through the airport the team was able to map and integrate the different flows. For each of these four journeys the team also mapped the different steps in detail – for example, passenger journeys through the airport were broken down into check-in, security and departure lounge.

Using the journeys as the basis for data collection, they then rated the performance of each step using a Red, Amber, Green system (RAG). This enabled them to monitor the whole customer journey and easily identify hold-ups and other problems. They could then focus on solving the issues as they arose or flag up the need for further analysis.

One of the key results that the passenger journey mapping and data collection process delivered was the realisation of just how many passengers had to change terminal for connecting flights. Most airlines belong to one of the major alliances in the industry and connecting flights are usually with airlines from the same alliance. But the airlines at Heathrow were not clustered in alliance groupings so up to 70 per cent of passengers making connecting flights had to change terminal to do so. The new Terminal 5 helped to resolve this problem, as it allowed BAA to cluster the main alliance partners and their agents more efficiently. By 2008 only 30 per cent of passengers had to change terminals to catch their connecting flight. The result of this major change, plus many more incremental changes to the customer journey (based on the data collected) was that Heathrow had jumped to seventh place out of 13 when it was benchmarked against other European airports in 2009.

(Source: Brown and Gilbert, 2010)

QUICK QUIZ – CHECK YOUR KNOWLEDGE

Questions
1. What are the four ways in which value added can be measured, according to McDonald and Wilson?
2. What is the difference between a Critical Success Factor and a Key Performance Indicator?
3. Why should organisations try to avoid strategic drift?

Answers
1. Value Chain analysis, SVA, Customer Value, Accounting Value.
2. CSFs are the elements or activities that are crucial to success, and KPIs are the measures by which these elements can be assessed.
3. It makes them less able to respond to major changes in the environment and it can mean that their strategy is developing incrementally through practice rather than in a planned and responsive manner.

FURTHER READING

Books
Core text:
Hooley, G., Nicoulaud, B., Piercy, N. and Rudd, J. (2017) *Marketing strategy and competitive positioning*. 6th edition. Harlow, FT Prentice Hall. Chapter 1.

Supplementary texts:
Aaker, D. and McLouglin, D. (2010) *Strategic market management: global perspectives*. Chichester, John Wiley. Chapter 6.

Cravens, D.W. and Piercy, N. (2012) *Strategic marketing*. 10th edition. US, McGraw-Hill. Chapter 15.

McDonald, M. and Wilson, H. (2016) *Marketing plans: how to prepare them, how to profit from them*. 8th edition. Chichester, John Wiley. Chapter 13.

References
Bolton R.N., Gustafsson A., McColl-Kennedy J., Sirianni N.J. and Tse D.K. (2014) Small details that make big differences: a radical approach to consumption experience as a firm's differentiating strategy. *Journal of Service Management*, Vol25(2), pp253-274.

Brown, P. and Gilbert, A. (2010) *High flyers*. British Quality Foundation. [Available at www.bqf.org.uk]

Chaffey, D. and Smith P. (2013) *Emarketing excellence*. Oxford, Butterworth Heinemann.

Johnson, G., Whittington, R. and Scholes, K. (2011) *Exploring strategy*. Harlow, FT Prentice Hall.

Kulpinski, M.E. (1992) The planning process – continuous improvement. *Journal of Business and Industrial Marketing*, Vol7(2), pp71–76.

Parmenter, D. (2007) *Key performance indicators: developing, implementing, and using winning KPIs*. Chichester, Wiley.

FEEDBACK TO ACTIVITIES

ACTIVITY 1.1 (SEE P21)

Using the case study above list the key factors in the automotive industry's macro environment that are likely to have an impact on firms in this sector over the next five to ten years. How are these factors interrelated? Rate each of the factors you have identified relative to the others, perhaps by using a scoring system. For example +3 = highly favourable factor – so a potentially good opportunity for the organisation, +2 = moderately favourable factor, -1 = slightly unfavourable factor – so could represent a minor threat, -3 = highly unfavourable factor – a major threat, etc.. Which factors are most likely to have an impact on automobile manufacturers? We will return to evaluation techniques and extend this form of analysis further in Chapter 3.

FEEDBACK

Below is an example of the sort of factors you might have identified from the case study. There is scope to explore this aspect of the automotive industry's macro environment in much more detail. If you want to extend the analysis you could apply some of the techniques covered in Activity 3.2 from Chapter 3. You will see from the ratings in the middle column of the table that deciding if something is a threat or an opportunity is not always straightforward – context plays a part as does being able to manage uncertainty (again covered in Chapter 3's section on scenario planning). To give one example, the regulation of CO_2 emissions could be a significant opportunity for a company that has strong innovation capabilities and is good at reading the market – but for other manufacturers it may mean that they have to change their business model significantly and it could put them at a disadvantage.

Factor	Evidence and rating	Relationship with other macro-environmental factors
Political/ Legal	• Regulation of CO_2 emissions (+/-3) • Scrappage schemes (+2)	• Technological – reliant on new technologies such as electric and hybrid vehicles, which will help to reduce pollution. • Economic – linked to the global recession of 2008-10.

Economic	• Oil price fluctuations (-2) • Raw material prices (-3) • Interest rates (+/-2)	• Political – volatility in North Africa and Middle East among oil-producing nations. • Social – consumer attitudes to debt.
Social	• Decline in car ownership among young people in developed economies (-2) • Increase in car ownership in developing BRIC countries (+3)	• Economic – high growth economies, GDP and disposable income increasing.
Technological	• Robot/driverless cars (-1) • Alternative propulsion systems (+2)	• Legal - issues around insurance and fitness to drive will need to be tackled. Social acceptance of this technological innovation will also be an issue. • Political – being driven by CO_2 emissions targets.

There are many other factors that a wider survey of the automotive industry's macro-environment would uncover – but this exercise is intended to give a flavour of this and to show clearly the relationship between different factors.

ACTIVITY 1.2 (SEE P26)

Think about the organisation you work for or one that you know well. What approach does it take to analysing its external environment – is it reactive or proactive? You may find it helpful to canvass the views of some of your colleagues or staff who work for the organisation you choose.

FEEDBACK

Answers will depend on context – but most organisations use a mix of reactive and proactive approaches to analysing the external environment.

ACTIVITY 2.1 (SEE P34)

Think about a car journey from one city to another. What resources (assets) and what capabilities (skills and abilities) would you need to complete this journey?

FEEDBACK

In order to get from A to B you would need a car, fuel, probably a map or GPS, knowledge of the Highway Code (a basic understanding of the rules and laws governing the use of motor vehicles in the country in which the journey is taking place) and knowledge of how to drive a car. But in order to complete the journey and make use of these assets you would need to be able to drive a car and have some navigation skills.

ACTIVITY 2.2 (SEE P40)

Using the resource and capability categories listed above and the VRIN/O framework, identify Inditex's resources and capabilities and decide which of them support and sustain a competitive advantage over its competitors.

FEEDBACK

Resources	Evidence	Level of competitive advantage
Tangible Physical	• Co-location of designers, factories and distribution centres in north-west Spain.	• Valuable, rare and hard to copy (built up over 25 years). However, other firms may substitute this with virtual networks and the advantages gained by access to lower-cost production in Asia.
Financial	• Access to capital markets via public listing.	• Valuable, but other firms in the sector have access to funds.
Technological	• Technical processes that support small-batch production and short-run manufacturing.	• Valuable because they directly support the firm's business model. Were rare – but other fast-fashion retailers have started to copy this approach.

Organisational	• Systems that support gathering and communication of market intelligence by front-line staff.	• As above – valuable because they support the firm's business model, and possibly rare – though more research into competitors would be needed to determine this.
Intangible Human/ intellectual	• Ortega family's knowledge of the fashion business. • Diverse workforce representing over 150 nationalities, so knowledge of a wide range of national and regional cultures	• Valuable because it supports the business model. Rare – as first-movers in the fast-fashion sector they have developed a lot of knowledge over 25 years. Hard to copy – it is unlikely members of the family would join a rival. Hard to substitute using market research – but possible long-serving senior management teams might have this knowledge too. Used by the organisation – the knowledge is at the heart of the structure, systems and culture. • Valuable – gives the firm an understanding of the tastes and needs of different cultures – but other global fashion houses have this diversity .
Brands/ reputation	• Portfolio of high street retail brands – including Zara, Massimo Dutti etc.	• Valuable – underpin the customer value proposition. Rarity might exist for individual brands – but other fast fashion retailers have a portfolio of brands. Inditex's breadth might be considered rare and difficult to copy.

Resources	Evidence	Level of competitive advantage
Relationships	• Supply chain relationships within Spain and North Africa. • Internal relationships between different functions within the business.	• Valuable – underpin the operating model. Rare – most competitors source in Asia. Hard to imitate – due to social complexity and time over which the relationships have developed. • Valuable – supports effective operating model with fast new product development. Rare – especially when coupled with the co-location asset above. Possible to imitate at a reasonable cost.
Culture and incentive systems	• Culture that supports/ encourages innovation and feedback from employees.	• Valuable – underpins the operating model and customer value proposition. Rare – distinctive culture. Hard to imitate – socially complex, development over 25 years, unique to Inditex. However, other cultures in fast fashion rivals may have developed differently and provide a viable substitute
Ability to manage a portfolio of retail fashion brands on a global basis.	• Ownership of a range of brand names and successful operation of retail companies over a number of years.	• Valuable – core part of being able to deliver customer value proposition. Rare – no: other groups in fast fashion also manage portfolio of brands on a global basis.

Ability to innovate continuously.	• Fast turnaround and rapid new product development as well as changes to processes on an ongoing basis.	• Valuable – core to the business model. Rare – few companies are able to sustain constant change. Hard to imitate – rivals would have to change their business model and probably their location too (the capability is linked to the proximity of various parts of the business in Spain).
Ability to create and sustain a culture that supports innovation and employee involvement.	• Fast fashion business model is based on rapid new product development and relies on front-line staff helping the firm to respond to changes in customer demands.	• Valuable – at the core of the business model. Rare – seen as a source of competitive advantage by rivals. Hard to copy – yes: sustaining a supportive culture is a socially complex activity. Other organisational cultures could be seen as substitutes.

ACTIVITY 2.3 (SEE P51)

Below is a simplified profit and loss account and balance sheet for a company manufacturing and selling microscopy consumables.

Short accounts for Lion Components

Profit and loss accounts for the years ended 31 December 2012 and 31 December 2013

$million	2012		2013	
Sales		960		1,020
Cost of sales				
Materials	300		320	
Labour	160		162	
Distribution	130		133	
Depreciation/amortisation	90		90	
Promotion	120		130	
Plant overheads	80		80	
		(880)		(915)

Gross profit		**80**		**105**
Administration expenses				
Labour	26		36	
Loan interest	41		51	
Other expenses	3		3	
		(70)		(90)
Profit before taxation		**10**		**15**
Tax (20%)		(2)		(3)
Net profit		**8**		**12**
Dividend		(0)		(0)
Retained earnings		**8**		**12**

Balance sheet at 31 December 2013

$million		
Non-current assets		
Intangible assets	400	
Property, plant and machinery	680	
Less accumulated depreciation/amortisation	(300)	
		780
Current assets		
Stock	230	
Debtors	304	
Cash	76	
	610	
Current liabilities		
Creditors	483	
Tax	2	
Dividend payable	0	
	485	
Net current assets		125
Long-term debt		(460)
Net assets		**445**
Shareholders' interest		
437,000,000 ordinary shares authorised, issued and fully paid at $1	437	

Retained profit	8	
Equity		**445**

Using the formulas above, calculate the profit, liquidity and stock turnover figures for 2013. What do they tell you about the company? Calculate the net profit margin for 2012. How does this compare with the figure for 2013?

FEEDBACK

Profit
Net Profit Margin for 2013 = 12/1020 or 0.0117 or just over 1%. Investors would be well advised to put their money in other shares or a deposit account at a bank – it would pay better. However, the Net Profit Margin for 2012 was even worse – 8/960 or 0.0083 – so less than 1%.

ROCE = 15/(780+125) or 0.016 – a 1.6% return on capital employed. The company is underperforming substantially. Many businesses would look at 10-14% as an acceptable return. Even though Lion sells commodities rather than capital equipment this is still a very low return.

Liquidity
Current Ratio = 610/485 or 1.26. The company appears to be in a fair position from the point of view of being able to service its debts and manage its cash flow, as this ratio is above 1.0.

Acid Test = 610-230/485 – or 0.78. Once the stock is taken out of the equation the liquidity position does not look as good – below 0.8. Even for a company that sells consumables this is on the low side.

Inventory/Asset utilisation measures
Inventory Turnover = 915/230 or 3.97 – so the stock is completely sold about four times over the year. Coupled with the profit figures above it is clear the company needs to grow its sales substantially.

Days of Inventory = (230/915) x 365 or 91.7 days. This seems high for a manufacturer of consumables, and suggests scope for more efficient outbound logistics and sales and marketing.

ACTIVITY 3.1 (SEE P61)
Make a list of acceptable and unacceptable intelligence-gathering activities for your organisation. Would this list be different if you worked for another type of organisation (not-for-profit, government, commercial etc)?

FEEDBACK

It is generally accepted that headhunting rivals' key employees or interviewing them to gain insights into a competitor is par for the course in commercial organisations – although some countries regulate this. Similarly, talking to a rival's customers, mystery shopping or asking intermediaries to pose as buyers in order to gain technical information or performance data would be unlikely to cause much outrage in the media. However, some surveillance techniques, such as bugging (increasingly possible as the price of these products reduces) or using double agents, might be seen as unethical in many organisations. One useful test is to consider how the discovery of the intelligence-gathering techniques might be covered in the media.

ACTIVITY 3.2 (SEE P64)

Carry out a PEST analysis for an organisation that you're familiar with. Use the impact/predictability matrix to identify the key factors that you will need to research further.

FEEDBACK

This will depend on the context of the organisation you have chosen, but it should clearly show you the distinction between single-event PEST factors and those forces that are driving change in the environment.

ACTIVITY 3.3 (SEE P75)

Using the Nike case study, identify the company's resources and capabilities and estimate how strong they are compared with competitors such as Adidas and Puma and how important they might be in creating value for the firm's customers. Use the Portfolio Matrix above to plot each resource and capability you have scored. What does this tell you about the company?

FEEDBACK

Below are some of the resources and capabilities you might have noted down from reading the case study. Many of the resources are intangible so can be difficult to value accurately.

Resources
- Physical – retail outlets.
- Technical resources such as Swoosh trademark.
- Brands – Nike, Converse, Starter etc.
- Human resources – wide knowledge base due to in-house specialists.

- Relationships – with key athletes such as Michael Jordan and Tiger Woods.
- Cultural – innovative culture.

Capabilities
- Ability to develop innovative new products.
- Ability to manage 'open' approaches to innovation.
- Acquisition and management of a portfolio of brands.
- Strategic marketing management.
- Ability to spot future sports stars.

In terms of evaluating and scoring these resources and capabilities the results will be subjective to a degree – unless you're an expert in sports apparel and footwear. However, applying the VRIN criteria covered in Chapter 2 will give you a logical basis for your judgement. The capabilities are more likely to give Nike a competitive advantage and count as major strengths – for example, the ability to spot future sports stars is not likely to be an exact science, so will be complex and hard to define and therefore harder for rivals to copy. Similarly, the knowledge resources resulting from having so many in-house experts is also likely to be a key strength.

ACTIVITY 3.4 (SEE P77)

Source a SWOT analysis from your organisation or one that you know well. Apply Coman and Ronen's, and McDonald and Wilson's criteria to the factors within the SWOT. How well do they meet these parameters? (If you can't find a SWOT within your organisation there are many examples online. Just enter 'example SWOT analysis' or something similar.

FEEDBACK

This will depend on the context – the poorest SWOTs will tend to confuse the internal with the external (eg by listing threats under weaknesses, for example) and will be a long and vague list.

ACTIVITY 4.1 (SEE P84)

Look for objectives in a range of documents for the organisation you work for or one you have researched. Annual reports, shareholder briefings, business or marketing strategies and plans may all be useful starting points. Are the objectives in these documents SMART? If they are, look at how the different criteria are manifested. If the objectives aren't SMART, use the criteria to try to make them SMART.

FEEDBACK

This will depend on the context – but you are looking for the lack of or presence of focused objectives with details that match the five requirements. Where one or more details are missing you can add them in. The hardest element to judge in this exercise is the 'realistic' criteria: knowledge of the organisation and its context are important in assessing this in an objective.

ACTIVITY 4.2 (SEE P96)

Debate the following: are there ever situations where a differentiated product or service should be priced much lower than competitors?

FEEDBACK

Conventional wisdom is that this would ultimately undermine customers' perception of the product or service – so limited sales promotions might be feasible but otherwise it is a dangerous step to take. Some commentators suggest that it is a potential short-term response to aggressive low-cost entrants to the market.

ACTIVITY 5.1 (SEE P107)

Make a list of the activities you are currently working on and then score each of them for impact and effort (with 1 as the lowest and 10 the highest). Then plot them on an Action Priority matrix.

FEEDBACK

This will depend on the context. The effort element of the exercise is easier to generalise – thinking about the number of people involved, the time a project is likely to take, its complexity, number of objectives etc can all help to determine this. Impact is much more dependent on the nature of the organisation and its specific situation – however, relating the activities to organisational or personal objectives can give some indication of their impact.

ACTIVITY 5.2 (SEE P113)

Think about a project or plan that you have been involved with. Using the criteria above prepare a list of risks that could have had an impact on this project or plan. Make notes on the way that each of the risks might have affected the project or plan. Asking 'what if?' can be a useful way of doing this.

Again this will be very contextual, but it does link to some of the earlier topics in Chapters 1 and 3 – such as analysing the macro environment and scenario planning – so it is worth seeing if some of these tools can give you a good start in terms of identifying risk factors.

ACTIVITY 6.1 (SEE P129)

Choose two organisations – one should be a government or not-for-profit organisation and the other a commercial enterprise. Compile a list of KPIs/CSFs for each organisation (either by looking them up from organisational sources or by imagining what measures would be most important for each organisation). How do the lists differ?

FEEDBACK

The detail will vary according to the context, but commercial organisations are likely to have some focus on profit and investor returns whereas not-for-profit or government organisations will have a different set of financial backers and terminology for the financial aspect of performance measurement and control – surplus is a commonly used term instead of profit, for example. A lot of charities' KPIs are likely to stem from fundraising activity – so metrics around the gain and loss of donors and the amount of donations will be common. Other operational measures may look at trust or user satisfaction as opposed to market share, customer satisfaction or customer complaints.

149

ACTIVITY 6.2 (SEE P130)

Using a selection of measures from Fig 6.1 above – or from your own research into the topic – construct a marketing dashboard template for key marketing metrics in your organisation, or one you know well. Think about how this will link to the organisation's objectives.

FEEDBACK

This will depend on the context of the organisation. Cravens and Piercy give a sample dashboard on p460 of their book for a comparison.